In his book, *Finding God, Finding Each Other,* Dr. Vincent Ruhl shows just how this amazing power of God worked in his family's life, healed their relationships, and enabled them to reach out and share with others.

—Ruth Stafford Peale
Chairman of the Board, Guideposts

Dr. Ruhl's book is highly readable and will prove to be a great blessing to all struggling for faith. I recommend it highly.

—Ron Hembree
President, Good Friends Ministry

At a time when many married couples desperately need support and encouragement for their marriages, Vincent and Linda Ruhl courageously show how husbands and wives can draw on the power of God to enrich and restore their love. An inspiring, practical, and encouraging book.

—Father Paul Keenan
author, *Stages of the Soul:
The Path of the Soulful Life*

Finding God, Finding Each Other

*How Our Marriage Was Saved
by the Power of God*

Vincent Ruhl

THOMAS NELSON PUBLISHERS
Nashville

Published in Nashville, Tennessee, by Thomas Nelson, Inc.

Scripture quotations are from the KING JAMES VERSION.

Library of Congress Cataloging-in-Publication Data

Ruhl, Vincent.
    Finding God, Finding Each Other : how our marriage was saved by the power
of God / Vincent Ruhl.
    p. cm.
    ISBN 0-7852-6773-5 (pbk.)
    1. Ruhl, Vincent. 2. Husbands—United States—Biography.
    3. Christian biography—United States. I. Title.

BR1725.R84 A3 2001
277.3'0828'0922—dc21
[B]   00–055414

Printed in the United States of America
1 2 3 4 5 6 QWD 05 04 03 02 01

This book is dedicated to
my wife, Linda;
my children, Jason and Sarah;
and my parents, Albert David and Rose.

Contents

ACKNOWLEDGMENTS

Thanks to Linda and Sarah for their input, encouragement, prayer, and vision that this would be a great book.

Thanks to Jeanne Cavelos for editorial work on the original manuscript.

Thanks to Ceil Canobbio for persistent prayer.

Thanks to Victor Oliver, Cindy Blades, and the cohesive team at Thomas Nelson for bringing this work to a place of excellence.

Thanks for wonderful reviews and endorsements:

Ron Hembree, President, Good Friends Ministry

Father Paul Keenan, best-selling author

Ruth Stafford Peale, Chairman of the Board, Guideposts

Dr. Lawrence Kennedy, President, COTR-International

Mary Elberfeld, Women of Substance Ministries

Thanks for prayer:

Pastors Richy and Cathe Petrello, Glory Zone Fellowship

Nick Della Valle, Crystal Cathedral Ministries

Dave and Joyce Meyer, Joyce Meyer Ministries

Ron Hembree, Good Friends

Thanks for encouraging support: Elizabeth, Sylvia, Pastor Herb, Roseanne, Dominick, Pastor Al, Mary, Rich, Pastor Dennis, Michelle, Laurie, Lorraine, Danny, Adrienne, Pastors Nate and Ronnie, Gina, Corrine, Fred, Jo-ann, Pilar, Wayne, Ronnie, Stella Mare, Pastor Janet, Hedy, and Father Tom.

Thanks to Jason for being my friend.

For thus saith the high and lofty One that inhabiteth eternity, whose name is Holy; I dwell in the high and holy place, with him also that is of a contrite and humble spirit, to revive the spirit of the humble, and to revive the heart of the contrite ones . . . I . . . will heal him . . . I will lead him also, and restore comforts unto him.

—Isaiah 57:15, 18

INTRODUCTION

During 1983 and 1984 my wife, Linda, and I had several incredible visions of God in the heat of a volatile and painful separation. Our relationship was saved by the power of God and dramatically restored.

The story in this book describes how I changed from a man consumed with selfishness, pride, and denial to one filled with love, humility, and integrity. It contains my wife's transformation as well. Although we each had to take our journeys alone, we would get a glimpse of the changes in the other, until eventually, like two vines, we became intertwined, traveling along the same path.

Finding God, Finding Each Other shares a love that is both divine and expressly human in the intimacy of marriage. It is also a story about the ways of God and how far He will go to help us if we just ask.

ONE

THE VOID

In the summer of 1982, Linda and I were upwardly mobile psychologists in our thirties. My strengths were cognitive behavior processes and applied behavior analysis. I was always trying to figure out how people worked. Linda was a developmental psychologist. She enjoyed helping handicapped people and had a great intuitive sense. We both worked at the Long Island Developmental Center, treating patients with developmental disabilities.

Linda and I had good jobs, and though we weren't yet married, we shared a beautiful house in the heart of Dix Hills, an affluent Long Island suburb. The road we lived on was unique: Vermont-like, woodsy, quiet, and isolated. We had been together for seven years and seemingly had everything going for us. I had formed a strong bond with her son from a previous marriage, Jason. I had sounded Linda out about marrying me, but she said she never wanted to marry again. I was willing to accept that for the time.

Even so, Linda and I were considered an ideal couple by those who knew us. She was from a Jewish background, and I had been raised as a Christian. My mom was Catholic, and Dad was Protestant. Despite our religious differences, Linda and I had an apparent unity because we both had scientific mind-sets. We participated in seminars, workshops, and psychological conventions in the northeast. Weekend trips to Boston, Philadelphia, Washington, D.C., and New York City were stimulating and fun. During our jaunts Jason enjoyed the opportunity to spend a few days with his grandparents in Queens. Linda and I got along well and did everything together. That's why her revelation that summer was such a blow.

We had first met in the computer center at graduate school. Although I was an earnest student and had come to the center for assistance, I couldn't help but notice Linda's creamy, clear complexion and well-defined cheekbones. She had a classy, simple look with understated makeup, wavy light brown hair, and hazel eyes that were soft and bright. I immediately concluded that she was a good-looking woman, my type; definitely my type. We were both average height, trim, athletic, and purposeful, spurred on to complete our psychology work. I was physically drawn to her. She was the research assistant in the lab, and I was trying to get as much information as possible out of her. It wasn't long into our conversation before she was giving me the business. "I'm not going to do your homework for you," she said. Her no-nonsense assertive approach and vitality attracted me more, and we quickly became closer. We initially spent hours, then entire days talking. We naturally enjoyed spending most of our free time together. We were intellectually suited and balanced each other emotionally. She was rather stoic and serious, while I was mellow and easy-going. Although we were both highly motivated, goal-oriented people, I was generally relaxed and content with an optimistic view of the big picture, whereas Linda was a bit pensive and driven by perfectionism. She was always on go, never really at rest.

We were both searching. I was searching through psychology for some kind of truth to center my life around. After I met Linda, she soon became my center. I thought she was going to be the answer to everything for me. I thought she was all I needed. Methodically, I made a plan: *Get Linda, make her happy.* After that, my plan was a little vague.

Our relationship blossomed and developed as I had hoped. I wanted to do everything with Linda. We rode horses and played tennis with each other. We loved films, concerts, and dance. Linda and I were both gourmet cooks. She specialized in fish and regional Chinese, while I was pretty good with northern Italian as well as French provincial. Wonderful afternoons were spent finding that special kitchen gadget or searching out provisions for a particular dish. Day excursions to neighboring Chinatown, Little Italy in New York City, or the Hamptons on Long Island were routine. We shared a beautiful garden of herbs that were picked fresh in season and dried for winter use.

I had believed that people in love should do everything together. When Linda wouldn't watch football with me, I gave up watching it. She would set goals for us, and I would carry them out. It seemed like a perfect partnership. However, I was discarding my own needs and identity, for she had filled my life in a simple, deceptive way. I was afraid to look inside.

Linda was still searching, her quest progressing a little farther than mine. She was beginning to sense that nothing in her life could fill the emptiness she felt inside. Her first marriage had left some scars. When Jason was two and a half, her husband was paralyzed in a car accident. She went to the hospital to visit him three times a day for the three years he lived after the accident. He was hostile and abusive to her, but she couldn't stop herself from going. Like picking at a scab, she couldn't let the wound heal. She had to examine it, to touch it again and again in a desperate attempt at understanding. But none came. She had sealed it off and moved on. But as her relationship with me developed, a frightening awareness grew inside her. She was beginning to feel smothered by me, yet simultaneously empty inside. She had thought, *If I forget my ex, I'll be happy.* But she wasn't. She'd thought, *If I go back to school, I'll be happy.* But she wasn't. She'd thought, *If I earn my degree, I'll be happy.* But she wasn't. She'd thought, *If I can find a lasting relationship with a man, I'll be happy.* But she wasn't. She'd thought, *If I get a house, I'll be happy.* But she'd gotten all of those things, and she wasn't. Quiet desperation had been building in her for years. She had reached a stone wall.

And it was one afternoon in late June, after we had been together seven years, when she decided to tell me this. Jason, who was thirteen at the time, was home and we were driving to the riding stable where Linda boarded our elegant gray show horse, Quarter Moon. The day was sunny and clear, and the landscape around us was bursting with life and health.

On some level I must have noticed that Linda seemed quieter and less happy recently, but I easily buried all that under the determination that I was making her happy.

Linda looked great in her jeans and with highlights glistening through her hair. She turned to me. "Vinnie, I have to tell you something. Something is wrong. I'm not happy at all."

I felt as if she had personally attacked me. "What?"

"I don't think I'm clinically depressed. I mean everything is fine." She ticked off the points on her fingers. "I have a great job. Jason is healthy. I have a beautiful home and my dream horse, Moon, that I always wanted." She dropped her hands. "I'm just not happy. I think I need therapy. What do you think?"

My anger was building rapidly. "Are you crazy? You are the second-best psychologist in Suffolk County, right after me, and if you need therapy, I'll do it. But you know very well that therapy is not the solution to your happiness."

Linda's eyes held mine. "Well, I need something. I feel empty inside. It's like a vacuum. There's nothing there."

I was an expert at evading truth and putting my own spin on things, but she had stopped me dead in my tracks. I felt the exact same emptiness within myself, but I was unwilling to acknowledge it.

Despite my denial, her statements had shaken me. My plan was a failure. I was a failure. I had gotten Linda, but she was not happy. We were growing apart, and my life was losing its center. I kept my emotions carefully buried and worked to evade this truth. Shallow platitudes came out, and eventually I got Linda to drop the subject. On the surface it seemed that we had resolved the subject. But my own feelings of anger and confusion would not disappear.

Weeks later we were sitting out on the slate patio in the backyard. Everything about our house was tasteful: from the custom-made glass doors to the patio and wrought-iron chairs, to the carefully arranged plants and patio stones, which Linda had envisioned and I had laid—under her careful scrutiny. We looked out on the surrounding woods.

I always loved the quiet privacy of our house, though she felt uneasy and afraid if she was home alone at night.

I had thought my plans through carefully since that day in the car, and now was the time to carry them out. I said, "You know, Linda, we don't always have to do everything together. You seem to be interested in certain things—your house, your horse. I'm not interested in that. I don't have time for riding anymore. I came this far to be trained to help people. I want to go further into therapy for others, develop my private practice, and you could work with me."

Linda flinched, and her whole frame stiffened. We both knew that I was the one who always wanted to do everything together and Linda the one who wanted more independence. But for me to come out in favor of more independence was a great strategic move for me. It put her on uncertain ground. And it helped me pull away from her pain. If I couldn't make her happy, then I'd let her be unhappy alone.

After a moment, Linda shrugged. "Fine. If you don't want to ride, I can go by myself. I've done it before. You know I don't want to go into private practice, though. I like working at the hospital."

I did know that. In fact it was part of my plan, though not in a conscious, deliberate sense. But in my subconscious I knew that the conversation in the car had signaled the beginning of the end. I knew that the problems had been building for a long time, and that they were problems inherent in us, in our selfishness and in the void that we had both hoped to fill with each other. Those hollow spots within us were causing the uncertain ground that our relationship was built on to shift and collapse. They had not been filled, merely covered over, and they would not support us any longer. Eventually, there would be a cave-in, and we would come face-to-face with the emptiness.

Consciously, what I felt was a strong desire to distance myself from Linda and to protect myself from the crisis that I sensed was coming. I didn't want to know the truths that my subconscious knew. I wanted to stay as far away from them as possible. For some time—even before the conversation in the car—I had felt a growing attraction to Julie, a cotherapist who worked with me at Long Island Developmental Center. Julie was lively, intelligent, and dedicated. She was twenty-eight, a few years younger than me, slender and tall, with long straight blonde hair that she wore parted in the middle. She looked up to me in a way that Linda didn't, and I found it very appealing. I found myself fantasizing about Julie constantly. I knew that she was attracted to me, and that I only had to say the word. I had known that Linda would not want to go into private practice with me, but by asking her and having her turn me down, I now had cleared the way to announce in a few weeks that I was going to ask Julie to be my partner in my professional practice.

Fall came and went, with Julie and me making plans for our private practice and growing closer than ever, and Linda becoming more depressed and distant. The collapse of our relationship was nearly complete, and I didn't want to be there when the walls caved in. Finally, in February I had to act. We were standing in the dining room, where Linda was pointing out some streaks in the paint job I had finished the week before.

I had planned this speech a dozen times, and now I suddenly forced myself to speak. "Linda, I have to talk to you about something important." She turned to me and made eye contact. I had difficulty looking into her trusting gaze. I forced myself to continue. "I don't love you anymore. It's not really that I don't love you—it's like you're my sister, we're friends. There's no romantic attraction between us. I'm going to leave. I need to get my own place."

Linda cried out, "Oh." It was a soft, wounded sound.

Her reaction was not what I had expected. I guess that I had wanted her to become angry and attack me. Then, in the midst of a fight, it would be easier for me to leave and to put most of the blame for our breakup on her. But she didn't get angry.

"Give me another chance," Linda said. Her face was blank. She was taken totally off guard. She hadn't had a clue this was coming.

"You don't understand," I said. "You haven't really been

present here for a long time. You don't want to be with me."
True to form, I shifted the emphasis from my desires to
hers, making her the source of the problem rather than me.
This was my specialty. And she bought it.

"I do want to be with you," she pleaded. "I'll try harder
to make the relationship work."

"I just need to be alone," I said.

"You mean you want to go off for awhile and reflect on
your life, think things over?" Now it was Linda's turn to
shift the emphasis, from my leaving her permanently to my
leaving her temporarily to think things over. This was not
really accurate, but at the time it was much less painful for
both of us, so we latched onto it. Linda's desperation to
hold things together gave my approaching-middle-age male
ego a boost, while this shift allowed me to avoid the messy
confrontation I had feared.

"Well, yes," I said, "I plan to spend a great deal of time
in solitude. A sort of retreat to sort things out, reflect on my
purpose."

Linda took a step closer to me. "You don't have to get
your own place to do that. You can do it right here."

"No, I have to be alone," I said. "I have to get away by
myself."

Linda nodded, her expression grim. "You can go away for
the weekend and just see how it goes. See what comes up.
Then maybe you'll be ready to come back."

14

I realized that I had won, and I was nearly overwhelmed by relief and a momentary sense of freedom. I would not have to directly face the cave-in of our relationship. I would not have to expose the void in each of us. I was going to make good my escape. I gave her an encouraging smile. "That's a good idea. Yeah, I'll do it."

TWO

EVASION AND DENIAL

The Circle Motel was a far cry from a retreat setting. Linda, of course, had been correct; my own backyard was far more serene and peaceful.

The motel was on a main road with traffic going by constantly. The rooms were adequate but no more. The bedspread and towels were worn, and the brown color scheme was depressing. I realized how spoiled I'd been in the home Linda had so painstakingly designed for us.

The freedom I'd felt at escaping from Linda was still there, but it was beginning to take on a frantic cast now, as if I were running in place. I needed to create a whole new life for myself, and fast. I took as much time as possible hanging up my clothes and arranging my toiletries. Finally the time came, and I had to sit and reflect. My thoughts were racing. I had no true understanding of myself. I still felt the strong need to pull away from Linda, and the attraction to Julie, but as for the bigger picture of my life, it was all a mess.

I broke my great solitude on that first day and went across the street to a little Italian restaurant. It was early evening, and the restaurant was empty. It was simple but clean, with red-and-white-checked tablecloths and paintings of Italy on the walls. The owner, who also served as chef and waiter, greeted me. He was a stocky, balding man brimming with energy and zeal. Just looking at him tired me.

"Hi, come on in. You live in the area?" he asked.

"No," I said. I didn't want to talk. I realized I should have just had some pizza delivered to my room.

"I own the place," he said. "I'm Joseph. I'm the chef here." He shook my hand and led me to a table. "I can cook anything you want. Everything is fresh. Everything is homemade." His belief in himself and in what he was doing came through clearly. "I won't even give you the menu. Just tell me what you want, and I'll make it. Everything is reasonably priced."

A small part of his energy moved me. I began to feel slightly eager over my dinner. "Could you make mussels marinara?"

"No problem."

"And a salad, linguini with white clam sauce, and a glass of red wine. What do you have by the glass?"

He smiled. "Whatever you want. I have Carlo Rossi, Chianti, Barolo . . ."

"You serve Barolo by the glass? I'll have that." Barolo was my favorite and hard to get at restaurants in a single glass.

He brought the wine quickly and then hustled off to the kitchen. Before long he returned with the food. The plates were heaping and the mussels were plump. I was caught up in the experience. The wine was delicious and the food seemed the best I had eaten in a long time.

As I finished, he stood smiling a few feet away. Now I couldn't stop talking. "Your food is fantastic. This restaurant is a real find. How do you do it?"

"I love to cook. I only opened recently, but so far it's been very successful. In a half hour or so my help comes in and the place starts filling up. I was in the insurance business, but I loved to cook. I always wanted a restaurant." He looked around the room, his pride and satisfaction evident. "It's been my dream. I've had a few places, but they never worked. I tried to keep my insurance business and run a restaurant too, but you can't do it. You can't do this part time. I've learned a lot. You have to go for it or there's no point. You can't be divided with two things." He paused and repeated, "You can't be divided with two things. Before I opened this place, I left my other job. It's a question of priorities. I'm clear about my priorities now. Let me get you a cup of espresso."

I can see now that God was speaking to me that night, but at the time I didn't realize it. I was struck by Joseph's clarity, enthusiasm, and sense of purpose. I realized that it wasn't the size of his business that mattered, but the quality of the experience that he offered—which was extraordinary—and his own personal satisfaction. If I could only feel like that, surely the void would disappear.

As I returned to my room, the happiness of the moment faded, leaving only a few of Joseph's phrases echoing in my mind. *You can't be divided with two things . . . It's a question of priorities.* It had been a long time since I had encountered the truth. And I didn't want to encounter it now. Denial and evasion had gotten me this far, and I wasn't about to abandon them now. My mind shut down and I went to sleep.

In the morning Joseph's words remained, and I decided to interpret them in a way that was consistent with my plans. I shouldn't be divided between Linda and Julie. I should leave Linda for Julie.

At the end of the weekend I went home. I knew that I wanted to move out, but I needed to make a few weak attempts to reconcile with Linda in order to satisfy our agreement and to appease my guilt. Once the attempts didn't work out, I could share the blame with Linda.

As soon as I returned, Linda began to bombard me with questions. "What did you decide? What are you going to do? Are you going to leave me?" Her desperation was painful to see, and her efforts to make things better between us only repelled me.

By early spring 1983 I was moving into my own apartment. Linda helped me with the move. I didn't want her assistance, but I couldn't refuse. At least this way she could see where I'd be, which might help her cope. I chose a large, one-bedroom apartment in a luxury complex. Allegedly my purpose was still "to be alone to reflect." The deception had been fully adopted by both of us at this point. It caused Linda less pain to think of our separation this way, and it was very convenient for me.

Linda had asked me repeatedly why I was leaving her, and if there was someone else in my life. And I had repeatedly denied it, saying, "It's not because there's someone else." And that was true. I was not *leaving* her because there was someone else. There were other reasons. But there *was* someone else. My evasive skills pulled me through once again.

I never really got around to furnishing the apartment. There was a huge living room with a solitary plant in the far corner. I bought a small, butcher-block table for the dining room and three wooden chairs. I don't know why I bought three. One for me, one for Jason, and one for Linda when they visited, I supposed. But they were never invited, and I never intended to invite them. There might be a chair for me, a chair for Julie, and then, the third chair. Why not four chairs?

I felt very uncomfortable in that apartment. I never had a phone connected. I didn't want any friends to call me. I didn't want to hear their questions or judgments. The sense of freedom had quickly passed, and I began to sense an underlying emptiness that filled me with anxiety.

I had not simply wanted to replace one home with another, one woman with another. What if I couldn't make Julie happy? I realized that I wanted some major change in my life. I didn't want to depend on another person so much.

I saw that I was off track, off my purpose that had been to make Linda happy. But I had abandoned that in favor of helping others. Wasn't that my purpose, to help others? I knew that I had lost my focus, and that my work was starting to suffer. If only I could concentrate on helping others, my life would be fulfilled and the emptiness would leave.

Over the following weeks I played the game of false solitude while alternating dates between Linda and Julie. I became adept at delivering half-truths to cover what I was doing. I was slippery, difficult to pin down.

Julie was not happy, since she had thought we would live happily ever after once I left Linda. I did tell Julie I loved her, and she said the same to me, but when she asked me how I saw our relationship, I always said we were "special friends." I wasn't ready to commit to her. I would steer our conversations toward our joint practice, which we were building part-time while retaining our full-time jobs.

Linda needed my support, but I couldn't give it to her. My moving out wasn't the only problem she had to cope with. She was going through a difficult time at work. Positions were being reassessed and reorganized, and there was a good chance she would lose her job because of seniority factors. Her beloved horse, Quarter Moon, had been crippled by a nail in his hoof, and she couldn't ride him anymore. She felt as if her life was falling apart. The emptiness was spreading, and she could do nothing about it. I sensed that the cave-in was imminent and kept my emotional distance.

I was detached, covering my feelings with half-truths while I continued to shift my free time between Linda and Julie.

One time I had Julie drop me off down the street from Linda's. I told Julie, "I need to get some exercise."

When Linda answered her door, she asked, "Where did you come from?"

I told her, "I walked," which of course wasn't strictly false. She believed me, and I felt a twinge of guilt. I was beginning to see that half-truths are half-lies. I fought the realization, but my conscience was starting to rebel.

I found that I couldn't confide in anyone, including my mother. Mom was kind, honest, and knew me well. We were good friends. I had a hard time making eye contact with people, including myself in the bathroom mirror. I tried to picture myself in five years, and couldn't. Instead

Linda's image rose in my mind. She was in pain, and she said, "Jason came to me and said, 'What are we going to do, Mom? Daddy died and left us and now Vinnie left us.'"

Then Julie's image came. She was whimpering. I had fed her expectations and let her down.

I finally determined to actually try to deal with these situations and figure out what problems I faced. I had evaded and denied long enough. What I realized was that I was responsible for my life. I was responsible for what had happened. I was responsible for the quality of my relationships. If something was lacking, it was my lack. If problems existed, they were my problems. For a few minutes, I embraced complete responsibility. I felt that I was not born to run, but to fight and move forward. But to fight what and to move in which direction?

My behavior patterns with Linda had been destructive, and those patterns would be repeated with Julie or anyone else. If I truly wanted to help people, well, why not help Linda and Jason? Instead I had hurt them deeply. I had tried to make Linda happy. And failed.

This led me to the conclusion that Linda was defective, or that she had betrayed me. But the truth, I realized, was that the very notion that I could make Linda happy was ridiculous. Most people weren't perfectly happy. And the idea that I had the power to make Linda happy was filled with hubris. In addition, I saw that I wanted her happiness for me, to make me happy, not for her. This put an incredible burden on her. I had been afraid of rejection and had instinctively realized that if I could make Linda happy, I would never be rejected. I was finally beginning to become aware but not yet ready to confront these issues and change.

One night the doorbell to the apartment rang at about midnight. I was upstairs with Julie and hurried to pull on my pants and get down to the landing. It was Linda. She looked as if she had thrown on a jacket and some sweatpants, her hair mussed, her whole frame tense. She moved to come in, and I blocked the entrance with my body.

"Who's up there?" Linda asked.

"None of your business." I stepped outside and closed the door behind me. "What do you want? Why are you bothering me here?"

"You had a call from the wife of a patient," she snapped back. "He's drunk in the basement of his house, smashing the furniture with an axe."

Crisis intervention was one of my specialties, and I focused on getting some necessary information. "Did she—"

"You reek of alcohol," she interrupted.

"Never mind that. I need to know—"

"What were you doing up there?" Linda's voice was beginning to waver.

"Be quiet and answer my questions. This is a crisis," I said.

Linda's face went hard. "She told her husband that she was

calling you, and he calmed down. I told her that you were out and I would try to reach you, but that you might not be available. I didn't try to explain that you don't have a phone. She almost begged me to find you and have you go over to their house." Linda crossed her arms. "What were you doing up there? Is there someone up there with you?"

"Yes, there is."

She stumbled back a step and looked as though the air had been knocked out of her by a massive stomach punch. I expected her to yell, to attack. Instead she mumbled, "I'm outta here. I'll be seeing you." She turned and walked down the sidewalk to the car. Her posture was so completely changed I wouldn't have recognized her if I hadn't known that it was Linda. She had always been very erect, assertive, in control. Now, she was hunched forward, her chest caved in, and she swayed from side to side, gripping herself around her ribs, almost totally collapsed. My overwhelming sense was that she had been mortally wounded, broken. I thought of her beautiful horse, who had been crippled and could barely walk. Too late I remembered the injured horse, the possible loss of her job—the other blows she had so recently received. Those had been inconvenient for me, and so I had buried my knowledge of them. The image of her shuffling down that walk burned into me. I couldn't take my eyes off of her until she drove away. Then I forced myself to rush upstairs. I had to go to my patient.

THREE

SAVED BY THE POWER OF GOD

I hustled up the stairs and told Julie to get dressed to go with me to the patient's home for a crisis intervention. We had been seeing the couple for marriage counseling as well as treating the husband separately for his own problems.

We drove to their house and talked to them for two to three hours, helping them gain control and order in their home. I have little recollection of what occurred. I felt simultaneously with them and outside of myself, watching. The image of Linda remained with me. I knew I had to resolve this situation and then go to her. Yet I didn't feel frantic or upset. I felt strangely at peace.

We returned to the apartment shortly before dawn. I sat Julie down at the little table and calmly explained what had happened with Linda. I told Julie that I had to change our relationship. I still considered her special and wanted to be "special friends," but I wanted our relationship to go back to being a professional one. I was going home to see Linda. Julie began to cry.

"You can't do this," she said, looking to me for consolation. "Vinnie, you said you loved me."

"I'm sorry," I said. "I did love you when I said that. But I also love Linda. I feel I have to try to work things out with her."

"You made a commitment to me. We're building a business together."

It was true. Although I'd never explicitly promised her marriage or lifelong happiness, our relationship had been filled with implicit promises. We talked for at least an hour, Julie alternating between anger and despair. For the first time, I realized how much I had used her and hurt her. I wanted to make it better for her, but the only way I could do that would be to commit to her. And I now knew I could never do that. The worst thing was that I was the only one she confided in. For my sake, she had kept our relationship a secret from everyone at work and all her friends. She had no one to go to now for support.

I walked her out to her car. She had stopped crying, and I had assured her we would continue to work together both at the developmental center and in our private practice. Her face was slack, exhausted, but I had the feeling she believed I would come back to her.

I felt bad for Julie, but the sense that I was doing the right thing overwhelmed everything else. I had to try to make things better with Linda. "Good-bye," I said in a neutral tone. "See you in a day or so."

I left immediately for home, feeling a quiet assurance that the outcome of my visit would be good. I didn't understand why I felt this, since I knew Linda well and knew that, after what I had done to her, she would most likely not want to have anything to do with me. Yet a sense of peace remained. As I entered the house, Linda was in the kitchen and Jason was getting ready for school. I released a prolonged sigh, relieved to see her posture had straightened up. She seemed soft, at ease. Her countenance was glowing.

I entered the kitchen. "I'm sorry, Linda. I know that I hurt you, and I want to come home."

She turned to me, a little startled. She was in the middle of making a sandwich for Jason's lunch. She was different somehow. "Where were you all night? Why do you want to come home now?" Although she didn't seem happy to see me, her response was far milder than I had anticipated. In the seven years we had been together I had never seen Linda cry. She usually held back expressions of intense emotion with her stoic temperament. In the rare times that she was pressed beyond her limit, she would tense up, stiffen, explode with anger, and storm around for several hours in a direct confrontation with the situation. Now, she seemed relaxed, at rest, calm, and peaceful. She was thoroughly out of her usual character.

"I went right over to my client's house and was there almost until dawn." I hoped for a little sympathy, though I didn't deserve it. "I went back to the apartment, washed my face, brushed my teeth, and came straight over here."

"And where was your friend?" she asked.

"Well, she came with me to do the intervention. We rode back together, and then I told her I had to come to see you, that she and I were just friends." I noticed that with Julie I had said "special friends," while with Linda I said "just friends." My half-truths were still alive.

"I don't know," Linda said. "I don't know if I can trust you."

I took a step closer. "You can trust me. I promise you, I'm home for good, and you can trust me."

She turned back to the sandwich. "What about your special friend?"

She had somehow instinctively picked up on my terminology. "We're just friends," I answered. "We do have some clients we work with together. You can't expect me to stop seeing them." I touched her arm, and surprisingly, she didn't withdraw from the physical contact. I was startled because she didn't tense up or move away. "How are you feeling? I couldn't stop thinking about you all last night. You seemed wounded. Are you okay?" I purposely understated her hurt in order to minimize my responsibility.

She looked me straight in the eye, and I was captured by the power of her gaze. "I was crushed last night. I was totally crushed. I think I would have killed you if I hadn't been so completely broken. I drove away from there with such unbelievable pain it's hard to get the words out to tell you. I was crying hysterically—I don't know how I got home. I wouldn't wish it on anyone, it was horrible. I needed help so I called my friend Lynn to come over. You know how far away she lives. It took her hours to get here. I just kept crying hysterically. I was yelling out, 'I'm hurt! I'm in pain!' Thank God Jason was sound asleep. I tried to make coffee, but I couldn't figure out what to do with the grounds.

"Finally Lynn came. My whole jacket was soaked with tears, and words were spilling out of me. We were sitting in the dining room when it happened . . . Come over here. I'll show you where I was sitting." Linda led me into the dining room and pointed to her chair. "Right there. And Lynn was sitting there." She slipped into the seat, and I sat beside her. Linda continued, "Lynn was saying, 'Who could have been up there with him? You shouldn't have anything to do with him. Vinnie is a creep.'

"I was just crying and crying, and then it happened. Jesus appeared to me, right in the room, right there"—she

30

pointed into the air—"suspended, hanging on a cross. When I saw Him, I lost all sense of the dining room, of Lynn, of anything beyond Him. He looked directly, intensely into my eyes, striking eyes filled with incredible love and compassion—I can't adequately describe the power of it to you. But I couldn't look away. I could see He was suffering, yet He looked so calm, so kind. He looked down at me and said, 'Linda, forgive them. They know not what they do. Forgive them.' At that moment, I experienced the depth of God's love for me. His words were important, but our communication went far deeper than words. His gaze pierced me"—she brought her hand to her heart—"and touched me. Then gradually I became aware of the dining room again, and He was gone. I felt this overwhelming peace. My crying stopped instantly, and I was calm.

"I asked Lynn if she had seen Him, and she said, 'Who?'

"I said, 'Jesus. Right there.'

"Lynn said that she hadn't seen anything, but that it had seemed as if I was 'away' for a few seconds, in some kind of trance. I told her what had happened, and she didn't understand. But she did see that I was totally changed. In a second I'd gone from suffering to peace. All the pain had been lifted right off of me. 'I'm okay,' I said. 'You can go home now.'

"'What do you mean you want me to go?' Lynn said. She

was flabbergasted. "I told her again what had happened and said I was fine.

"'You sure you're all right?' she asked.

"I said yes, and she said that, although I was acting weird, she could see that I was fine. It was amazing."

I was stunned by Linda's revelation. She'd been brought up Jewish, though she hadn't been particularly religious since I'd known her. She was a scientist, a psychologist. She knew about shock and what it could do to a person. Yet even as I thought this, I knew it wasn't shock. She was relaxed and alert. Shock was different. There had been an enormous change for the better in her. Even so, I had to ask. "Do you think it could be shock?"

She smiled. "I know it's not. If I were in shock, I'd be numb. But I'm not numb. I feel empowered and energized to go on with my life. I'm more alive now than I've ever been. I knew when I saw Jesus that you would come back to me. And here you are."

The depth of the experience and the changes in her were undeniable. Before, she would never have allowed me to come near to her without several days of assurance and apology. Peace filled her. I could not evade or deny that truth. It seemed impossible that from the crushing pain she had felt could come such peace. But what I didn't know was that such pain combined with a cry for help are precisely the ingredients that can invite God into our lives.

The pools of peace in Linda's eyes both frightened and drew me. I knew that this peace was real. It couldn't be accounted for by any psychological analysis or theory. It had to be accepted.

HUMBLE AND CONTRITE

The wedding took place the next month, in June of 1983. Linda was exquisite in an off-white French linen dress. Jason was my best man, and Lynn was the maid of honor. The day was crystal clear, and the owners of La Marmite, a fabulous French/Northern Italian restaurant, allowed us to hold the brief ceremony in one of their dining rooms. A grand reception followed, filling the entire ground floor. Old friends, relatives, fellow horse lovers, and psychologists had all come to wish us well.

Linda's fear of marriage and her determination never to marry again had dissolved under the all-encompassing peace she felt. When I had tentatively raised the idea after our reconciliation, she had surprised me by agreeing.

I enjoyed the celebration and felt good about finally marrying Linda, though I felt somewhat detached from her and everyone else. Although Linda and I were slowly rebuilding our relationship, this God she had met was not very real to me. Her astonishing encounter with Jesus had brought her a tangible and long-lasting blanket of peace, but it was her peace. She spoke to God, and He spoke back. She claimed that He had shown her where and when to get her wedding dress prior to our decision to marry. She believed He had guided her to find our wedding rings, three interlocked gold rings, one of them white gold. She said that the white gold ring represented God while the other two symbolized the two of us held together by God. The dress was gorgeous and the rings were stunning in their simplicity. However, this was all foreign to me. I felt her peace but had none of my own.

For our honeymoon, we went on a cruise and took Jason. He had a separate cabin, quickly met some new friends, went his own way, and had a blast. We fluctuated between having a great time and fighting about our recent past, in particular, Julie. Linda was still hurting from my betrayal, and this was not a wound that could be covered over. It needed to be healed. While Linda in general was more at peace and calmer, her perfectionism tempered, God had not made her into some kind of happy robot. She was still human, with feelings, many of which we hadn't dealt with yet. And of course, I had my own problems. I hadn't fully let go of Julie. I still saw her regularly since we still worked together.

When we returned from the cruise, our fights grew stronger and longer. I didn't understand that Linda needed to be healed, and I perceived her anger as an attack rather than as a signal for help. In mid-July, I left home again.

Julie was there to comfort me, though again I would not commit to her. I used her shamelessly. I told her about everything that had happened with Linda, dumping my problems on her. I lived out of my car. I was dirty, sweaty, and covered with mosquito bites. I didn't understand why life had to be so hard or why I had to suffer like this. I felt emptiness threatening me. One night I called Linda from a pay phone. She wasn't angry. Her peace had returned, yet she was firm.

"I can't allow this anymore."

"I'm going to come over for the evening," I said.

"No," she replied. "I can't allow this anymore. I love you, but I'm not going to be involved in your mess anymore. I will pray for you and your friend. Good-bye."

She hung up the phone. I couldn't believe she had hung up on me. She had said what she had to say and then hung up. She was praying for me—*sure*. But I knew that she was sincere. She had said "friend" in a gentle tone, not "special friend," the attack words. She wasn't playing by the rules. She was supposed to yell, and I was supposed to yell back. She was doing what God had told her to do. I still didn't know much about this God, but it seemed that whatever He said to do worked. That call hit me like a ton of bricks and when I finally hung up on the dial tone, I was afraid. It was a different kind of fear than I had ever felt before. I had a new sense of the seriousness of what I was doing, and had done, and of my own guilt. I realized that there was something more important at stake than who won the next argument.

I perceived that Linda had broken out of the negative cycle of our relationship with that call. She had ignored her friends, who said I was a bum and that she should let me have it. She was praying for me. She was waiting for God's voice so that she could make her next move. She was not just one step ahead of me in the game. She had quit playing the game. The game was over.

Linda had refused to see me, so I popped over unexpectedly. I caught her coming down the stairs into the living room.

"Hi," I said. "I just came to say hello."

Linda sighed. "What are you doing here? You can't just waltz in here anytime you want to." She was calm, but I sensed a cutting edge of firmness in her voice.

"I had to see you. I was thinking that maybe we should have counseling or do therapy."

"If I need therapy, I'll go alone," she replied.

I decided to try another approach. I knew that Jason was at his grandparents' and that Linda didn't like being home alone at night. "I'll keep you company. I know you don't like to be out here in the woods alone. I can stay with you tonight."

"Not a chance," she shot back. "I was alone last night and did just fine, and where were you? I was sitting on the couch in the living room, and I was afraid. I begged God to help me. Almost immediately these bright lights lit up the backyard. The light was almost blinding. I went to the patio doors to see what it was, and I saw angels encircling the house. I can't even find the words to describe them. They were very tall and powerful and appeared to be human-shaped, with huge wings. They were incredibly bright and awesome, and at first I was terrified. But I could tell somehow that they were warriors and that they had come to stand guard over me and the house. My initial fear quickly gave way to an extreme, overwhelming sense of peace. I knew they would always be there and that they would keep me safe. Something inside me was changed by that knowledge. I knew in my heart that there is a loving God who cares about me and my fears, who is always here to comfort and protect me. I knew that I was completely safe. I basked in His peace for a while, and then I went to bed. I don't need you here to protect me. I have the angels."

I was so fixated on getting to spend time with her, I barely reacted to this incredible story. The less she needed me, the more attracted to her I was. "I want to see you. What are you doing? Are you busy?"

"Actually, yes," she said. "I'm going out tonight and I have to get ready."

"Where are you going?"

"If you must know," she stated, "I'm going to a tent revival off the expressway. George told me there's going to be a great evangelist there. I may see George there, but he's not sure if he'll make it. He's going to see if his family can go." George was a middle-aged therapy aide at the Long Island Developmental Center. He was highly respected by the psychologists, and Linda had spoken of his wisdom and spirituality often. He was one of the few people at work who had reacted positively to the accounts of her encounters with God.

"I'll go with you," I suggested.

"No," she said.

"I would like to go with you. Why not?"

With a little annoyance she said, "Okay. You can come with me."

I sat in the living room and waited while Linda got ready. I wanted to spend time with her, but had no interest in seeing the evangelist. Evangelists brought to mind images of Burt Lancaster in *Elmer Gantry*. But then I thought about Billy Graham for a few moments. He was a man of outstanding integrity. I concluded that all evangelists weren't bad.

At least George might be there, and I could meet him. He seemed by all accounts to be a great guy. At least we had something in common to talk about.

We saw the tent from the expressway, lit up with spot-lights. It was immense. The place was mobbed with people and cars. The air was hot and humid, and bugs swarmed around the lights. An impeccably dressed man courteously led us to two seats.

The crowd was a mix of Hispanics, Whites, and Blacks. Though my family was of Italian and German descent, I had grown up in a predominantly African-American neigh-borhood filled with churchgoers. So I felt fairly comfortable in this group. All ages were represented, and dress ranged from casual to formal. We got seats about halfway back, the stage looking distant and small. On each side of the stage stood a tall, rectangular-shaped wooden box. They looked like coffins standing on end.

There was music, singing, the introduction of priests and ministers from the Long Island area, followed by the evan-gelist. His sermon seemed repetitious and drawn out. It didn't make much sense to me. Many of the people became emotional, and when an invitation came to go up to the altar to give money, the majority of those present did so.

After everyone got back to their seats, the evangelist began to proclaim his message. He said that you could choose either life or death. He said that Jesus was the Son of God and that in order to choose life you had to receive Him and accept the work He did on Calvary. I thought, *What's Calvary?* I had some trouble understanding the message. The language was different, and many of the concepts and ideas were foreign, but I did my best to follow. Although he spoke for more than an hour, the time flew by. Near the end of his sermon, he explained that the two coffins onstage contained two men who had recently died. In one was a man who had received Jesus, and in the other was a man who had refused to accept Jesus. He made it sound as though the second man had been given a clear choice and rejected Jesus. He lost me with some talk about the resurrection. But then he said, "On that day, do you know what's going to happen?"

Boom! The coffin on the right side of the stage sprang open and the man jumped out, alive, and he ran up and down the aisles, shouting, "I'm alive. I'm alive!"

The other coffin remained shut.

The evangelist invited anyone who wanted to receive Jesus and choose life to come up to the platform. After a few seconds, I stood and approached the stage. Linda came also. It felt like the right thing to do. I wanted to be alive. When I reached the front, the evangelist prayed for me.

Linda and I left shortly after. I felt I had come very close to something, but the strangeness of the words and the ideas had kept me at a distance, preventing me from making a real connection. For the first time, though, I really wanted to make that connection.

The next weekend I went to Westchester to visit my

mother, Rose. She was a warm, short Italian-American woman in her early seventies. Mom was a strong Catholic who always emphasized doing what was right in the sight of God. Since my father had died, we'd grown very close, visiting each other often. But after my breakup with Linda, I'd been avoiding her. I expected her to be so glad to see me that she'd roll out the red carpet, but her greeting was cool. After saying hello, I told her I was going across the street to walk in the park. These last few days I finally had been willing to be alone, to reflect. Yet I couldn't stop my thoughts from racing. I was very disturbed and confused. I was still using Julie, confiding in her and seeking understanding. It was getting very hard to ignore the pain I was putting her through. Yet I couldn't completely stop seeing her—we worked together after all.

I wanted to see the truth. In the park, the playing, laughing kids seemed miles away. I took a deep breath, trying to calm myself. It seemed impossible. I found a bench and made myself sit down. I wanted to ask for help, but from whom? I closed my eyes and focused on slowing my breathing. My mind formed a mental picture of my Dad who had died several years before. He looked at me and said, "Vinnie, you're married to Linda."

His body flickered and reformed into the image of Jesus. He had light brown hair and a beard, and His white robe glowed with a calming light. I had never seen anyone so kind and so good. Jesus looked at me and said, "Vinnie, you're married to Linda." His voice was gentle yet firm. I guess I had asked Him to come into my life in that tent. Now He was here.

I had a sense of peace and tried simply to accept the experience rather than analyze it. I asked again for help, and the same images repeated themselves before me. I wasn't sure what to think about the appearance of Jesus. I didn't feel ready to talk directly to God, as Linda did. I wasn't sure if Jesus had actually appeared to me, or if my mind had created His image. The vision did not seem to have the overwhelming power Linda had described. But then, perhaps God knew I wasn't ready for that yet.

I returned to my mom's house and sat down to her usual feast. "What do you think about my situation?" I asked, hoping for sympathy. My mother was always understanding as well as truthful and direct.

"What situation?" she responded.

"My separation from Linda. You don't know what it's like. She can be very angry and uncompromising at times. I was thinking that I would spend a few days here with you."

My mother said sharply, "You're married to Linda. Go home to your wife and take care of your family." Her tone awoke me, and I recognized the same message I had heard twice before. There was no mistaking it or evading it. We ate, and then I returned to Long Island.

I pulled into the parking lot near home, turned off the engine, and asked for help. I asked for it silently, with all my heart and all my strength. I wasn't mentally depressed or down. I was in a grave state of honesty. I wanted finally to understand and accept the truth. I admitted that I had made a complete mess of several people's lives, including my own. I had hurt Linda and lied repeatedly to her. Any anger she felt was justified. I had been filled with arrogance and pride. Now I felt humble. It was an unusual sensation, but relieving in a way. I no longer had to cover everything up, to avoid the truth. I had let Jason down. I had lied to Julie and made promises to her that I never intended to keep. Though our private practice was my dream—my dream of helping people—I didn't think I could continue to treat patients with her. How could I, when the dream was built on Julie's pain? I was very, very sorry for all the damage that I had caused. I didn't deny, evade, or analyze, because at last I was ready to accept. I was completely sorry and asked sincerely, straining for help. I felt like a drowning man going down with my final breath.

I said in a desperate whisper, "God, what should I do?"

A still, small voice inside me replied, "You're married to Linda. Go home." The voice was peaceful and kind, yet it carried the authority of a command. I was filled with its peace and assurance.

I went home, brought in my bags, and started to unpack.

I knew that what I was doing was right. I was broken, humble, and contrite, yet I had the power to do something I never would have dared to do before.

Linda came into the bedroom and said, "What do you think you're doing?"

"I'm moving back in," I said.

"Oh no, you're not!"

"Yes, I am," I said, and I was calm. I was not playing my side of the game anymore. "I'm married to you." I was baffled at how following His voice worked. The same peace and certainty that I had just experienced in my car was released through me. Linda stopped. She became calm and accepted the statement. I thought, *Wow, this works!* I noticed that kindness was somewhat lacking in me and determined that I would have to work on that.

I decided to resign from work in January, resolved to finally have a genuine retreat. I was ready to sit still, listen to God, and change my life. I learned quickly that there was a major overhaul to be made from the inside out.

FIVE

FINDING GOD

January 1984 was a critical month for me. There I was sitting on the couch, out of work, feeling very guilty and humble, searching for the truth. I felt as if my heart was a broken vase that had held nothing but lies and had shattered to slivers under the pressure. At the same time, I felt a blanket of peace covering me, comforting me through the pain.

I was conscious of the presence of God in the room. When I could stop my thoughts from racing and be still, I knew that He was there. When I focused on His light, some peace penetrated my inner darkness. But the peace was short-lived and difficult to maintain. Most of my time was spent brooding over the pain I had caused and the mess I had made of other people's lives, including my own. Everything I had touched was polluted. I had thought I was a good man. But I had lost my way, followed my worst instincts. Offensive aspects of my personality had come out. I had been too proud, too selfish. I had lied, broken commitments, and ignored the pain of others. Now I felt as if I had nothing. I could not continue in my work. I had damaged the people closest to me. And I was so sorry; I felt a powerful desire for relief.

I took out Linda's Bible and read Job and Proverbs. The reading was laborious, but I decided to read through some of the proverbs again. I felt a need to read certain sections repeatedly. The words contained God's wisdom. I read that Solomon had asked for wisdom to help the people. I wanted to help people as well. I asked God for the wisdom to help them. As I continued to read, I found that these were living words. One section seemed to describe precisely the feelings of fear and emptiness I'd had in my apartment, and it went on to offer marital advice, telling me to keep away from Julie. I felt as if I'd hit the jackpot. It seemed that the Bible was speaking directly to me, describing my situation exactly. My choices, and their consequences, became clear. I had a great sense of temporary relief along with the illumination. I had come face-to-face with a piece of the truth I was seeking. I accepted this truth eagerly now, rather than trying to deny or evade it. It brought me some strength and peace.

I took a nap and awoke with the urge to redecorate. When Linda came home, I could tell she was astonished, though her reaction was reserved. "What did you do to the house?" she asked.

I pulled her into the room, as proud as any boy who had just caught his first fish. "I just moved a few of those plants around. Sort of balanced them and lightened up the room. How do you like it?"

"Well . . ." She paused. "It looks nice, I guess." Linda looked surprised, not only about the plants but about her own reaction. She was a perfectionist about everything in the house, and arranging and caring for the plants was one of her major endeavors. She had found the perfect place for each plant, based on aesthetics, sunlight, and height. I had moved them around and she sort of liked it, an uncharacteristic response. Something had changed in both of us. A few months ago I would never have moved the plants, and if I had, she would not have liked any alterations.

"The plants look good," Linda said, raising a hand to her chin. "Maybe we should paint the rooms."

I hated painting; it had been the source of many arguments in the past. "Do you really think the rooms need painting? They look pretty good to me."

"The living room and bedrooms haven't been painted since we bought the house six years ago."

She was right, and I realized I'd have to resign myself to doing it, but I didn't want to talk about it anymore. I pulled Linda's hand away from her face and kissed her. She kissed back. One thing led to another. But afterward, as we lay side by side on the bed, I felt tension between us.

Linda broke the silence abruptly. "Did you ever do that with her?"

"Do what?" I replied, my eyes on the ceiling. "I don't want to talk about it."

"Then you did."

"No."

She turned to me. "Then what did you do? I want you to tell me."

"No."

She took my head and turned it toward her. "I want to know exactly what you did."

I gave in and shared some specifics of what Julie and I had done in my apartment.

She exploded, sitting up in the bed. "How could you have done that? I don't believe you anyway. I don't trust you. I don't care what you did."

I didn't know what to do. I had thought that perhaps by being totally honest I could regain her trust. But it didn't seem to be working. I was annoyed and unhappy with the way things had gone, but I was not yet shaken. Something was different. I knew that I was married to Linda. That voice came, and with it was a sense of permanence and assurance. I was married to Linda, and denial or evasion were not options.

Annoyed, I made a halfhearted attempt to soothe her, running my hand down her arm. "Don't think about the past. I'm here. You can trust me."

She jumped out of bed. "I'll never trust you. I'll get you for what you did. You're going to pay!"

Her threats pushed me over the edge. I slid across the bed and got up on her side, leaning right into her face and yelling. My arms were bent and ready to defend myself if necessary. "Now we see the real Linda! You're sick. Don't you ever threaten me." I wanted her to back down.

Linda pushed me.

I instinctively grabbed her and spun her around, trapping both her arms behind her and locking her up in a grip I'd learned to use on assaultive clients.

"That's it!" she screamed, struggling against me. "Now you're physically abusing me. I will not tolerate this. It's over. I will not tolerate physical abuse. Let me go. Let me go!"

I released her, feeling something had gone horribly wrong.

"I'm getting Jason and leaving. I'll sleep at a friend's." She stormed around the room, snatching up some clothes. As she headed for the door, I blocked her way. She picked up a large bottle of perfume and hefted it as if she were going to throw it at me.

"That's right, run off, go ahead, leave, good-bye," I snapped. "That's right and don't forget to wake Jason up and ruin his sleep. He has school tomorrow. Great mother, waking him up out of a dead sleep and dragging him into this."

Linda lowered the perfume bottle. "You watch him. I'm leaving. Get out of my way."

I stepped to the side and she pushed past me. Her steps pounded down the stairs, and I heard the garage door slam. The car engine raced briefly, and then she was gone.

How had things gone so wrong? The tables were turned this time, me at home and Linda gone. But I was different now and getting the upper hand was not the issue. I sat back down on the bed, humble and contrite. She was hurt, and I was guilty. The attack had arisen out of an unhealed wound that I had inflicted. I tried not to defend or intellectualize, though a few defensive thoughts did creep in. She had accused me of abusing her. I examined myself and decided that no, the desire to maim her had definitely not been present. I was too broken to have even a thread of denial running through my system. I had wanted to intimidate her and win the argument, but I hadn't had any intention of striking her. I'd grabbed her because I'd been annoyed and wanted to get her under control, but she was not an assaultive client and the action was wrong. Acting on my annoyance was wrong. Using physical force was wrong. Guilty as charged, again. I felt sorry and ashamed. I missed her and hoped she was okay.

Forty-five minutes later I heard her car. Linda came up the stairs.

"I'm sorry, Linda, it's totally my fault," I said. "I was annoyed and I allowed things to escalate. I was wrong. I'm sorry. I apologize."

Startled, she halted in the doorway. "You hit me. Don't ever try that again."

"I did not hit you," I firmly responded.

"You hit me. If you ever hit me again I will leave you for good. Do you understand?"

"I did not hit you," I repeated.

"Yes, you did," she challenged.

"No, I did not."

She started storming around the bedroom, picking things up. I realized the whole negative pattern was starting again. Being right was not worth it.

"I'm sorry," I said. "It's totally my fault. I shouldn't have grabbed you. I shouldn't have been so threatening. I'm sorry. I was wrong and I apologize." I wasn't pleading or being manipulative. I felt sincere.

Linda turned to me. "See that you don't do it again," she said. She began to undress, calmed. "She's going to call you, you know."

I hadn't heard from Julie since leaving work. I wondered where she'd gotten the idea but decided not to question it. "It doesn't matter. It's over for me."

She climbed into bed.

I lay beside her, looking straight up, and thought to myself, *Hmm, that worked.* No male ego. I apologized, and she accepted. I got it. But it wasn't a technique. I really was sorry. Out of my brokenness and understanding of my own imperfection, I really didn't care about being right. I'd never acted like that before, and she had never reacted like that before. It really seemed to work. I rolled over next to Linda, put my arm around her, and fell asleep.

Peace lasted for a few days. We didn't rehash it, analyze it, or discuss it. I spent part of each day just sitting down quietly on the couch with God. At times I read the Bible. The words of God were starting to take root in my plowed-up heart. But this Jesus—I had serious doubts about Him. I had drifted far from my Christian upbringing. Jesus said He was the only way, and I had a hard time with that. Certainly Jesus was one of the most enlightened people who had ever lived, greater even than Buddha. Jesus had felt love for His enemies as they tortured, degraded, and killed Him. He had achieved perfect peace in a brutal death. I realized that He was the ultimate example of enlightenment. But still, believing that He was the only way didn't fit into the shattered remnants of my belief system.

I sat and focused on the light. I read. Inside myself I felt pockets of infection and pollution surrounding a frightening darkness. I wanted to cleanse that infection; I wanted to get rid of the turmoil. I wanted to ease the pain and guilt. At some point it no longer mattered whether Jesus was the only way or not, just as it hadn't mattered who was right in my argument with Linda. At that time the real issue for me was whether Jesus worked. I needed relief. I had to have something that could drive away the tormenting emotions that plagued me again and again.

Several days after my fight with Linda, one morning while I was home alone, the phone rang. I pushed myself off of the couch, feeling weak and vulnerable. "Hello?"

"Vinnie, it's Julie."

Linda's prediction suddenly jumped back into my mind. I had forgotten all about it.

"Are you there?" Julie asked.

"Yeah. Hi." I didn't want to deal with this. I wanted to be able to move on and forget about what I'd done.

"How are you?" Julie's voice sounded small, lonely.

"I'm doing fine."

"So you don't miss me at all, I guess."

I couldn't imagine what the right thing to say might be. "Linda and I are working on our marriage."

"You said you loved me," Julie said angrily.

"I'm sorry. People change."

"Well maybe you'll change back again." I could feel her hurt through the phone, hurt I had caused. But encouraging her would only hurt her more.

"I don't think so."

"I still think about you, Vinnie. Keep me in the back of your mind. When you make spaghetti, think of me." She knew I loved pasta. I felt that she was trying to manipulate me. I became angry and I resented her attempt to make me keep thinking of her. It was Linda's thinking of her that was causing all the problems in our marriage. "I really don't want to think of you when I make the spaghetti. Goodbye." I hung up, my whole body trembling. I felt like I was walking a tightrope. It was the last time I spoke with her.

Not only had I hurt Linda, I had hurt Julie too. I was responsible for a lot of pain. And what could I do about it? It had been my resolve to make Linda happy that had gotten me into trouble in the first place. I couldn't be drawn now into trying to make Julie happy. Yet I had made her miserable. My guilt haunted me.

It lasted a few more days, my peace with Linda wearing thin. My heart was not healing. The guilt and torment were becoming more oppressive and pervasive. The only escape I could find from my pain was to put the blame on others. Old hurts and resentments kept resurfacing. I thought that Linda didn't appreciate me, that she had cared more about her horse than me, that she took and took and never gave. And then I thought about all the lies I had told her and how much I had hurt her. I felt like a parched wasteland, thirsty for a drop of water, craving for just a moist crumb of a cure, some balm that could ease my terrible ailment. Sitting on the living room couch, looking out the large window in the back, across the patio, and then up into the bright blue sky full of cumulus clouds, I cried out to Jesus for help. "Help me Jesus, please help me," I repeated. Begging silently, I thought, *If You're real, then show me that You work.* Then I wept for an interminable amount of time with a gut wrenching fervency as I bowed my head and shook it slowly in painful motions. When I looked up again . . . I saw Him suddenly, at the top of a mass of clouds. His face was as large as the cloud below Him, and His expression exuded compassion. He was beautiful and calm. I was drawn toward Him. His eyes were the deepest, most vivid blue. The color was penetrating yet soft at the same time. I felt swallowed up in it. And He was crying along with me. A tear ran down his cheek. His presence, His compassion, touched me.

In that moment, my guilt was lifted from me. I knew that I was forgiven. I felt suddenly light and free, like dancing, and I did a little jig in front of the couch.

Now I knew that Jesus worked. No one, nothing could negate my experience. I had seen Him. And He had showed me, all right. The bottom line was an absolute, unconditional forgiveness that surpassed any rational understanding. Jesus had the ability to completely forgive. His very presence released a flood of forgiveness without a word being spoken.

The experience was so private and personal that I didn't even share it with Linda. But I had finally met the God that Linda knew so well. I knew that my colleagues would say this was a *folie a deux*, a delusion shared by two people, but I knew better. Delusions don't work. Jesus worked. I marveled that Jesus was not demanding or controlling in any way. I had not yet invited Him into the innermost chamber of my heart, but He wasn't pushy. Instead, He had demonstrated His compassion and kindness, and then let me be. But seeing Him had sparked a flame of longing in me to have a closer relationship with Him.

SIX

HEALING

Linda picked silver flake, white lace, and bone as the three colors for our bedroom, the guest bedroom, and the living room. We both tried to approach the painting job with the idea that it would be easy and fun, hoping that it would not degenerate into a fight as our previous painting jobs had. In the past it had been my job to paint and Linda's job to inspect. This had been the source of many of our fights. Linda was a perfectionist, and even the wallpaper hanger who had come a few years ago had called her "eagle eye." In any home project, she was very difficult to please, immediately drawn to the slightest flaw. In fact, she often seemed on a mission dedicated to finding flaws. Perhaps I should have been more concerned about how this tendency had affected her, rather than how it had affected me. But although I had recently been receiving some divine understanding, I was not nearly to the point where I was able to freely give away much compassion and kindness.

A while ago we had painted the dining room, and Linda found a roller mark that could be seen only if you looked at a certain angle under certain lighting conditions. The job was much better than average, but that roller mark was there. After several do-overs with the finest roller money could buy, the job had been done. The roller mark was gone. Nevertheless, there had been no elation, no moment of pleased satisfaction. She had simply acknowledged that the job was finished, out of the way.

We pushed the bedroom furniture into the center of the room and spread drop cloths over the floor. We were both wearing our sloppy painting clothes, and Linda had a baseball cap on. She beamed, a broad smile on her face.

"How do you want to do this?" I asked.

"I don't know," she replied. "How do you want to do it?"

"Well, what would you like to do?" I asked.

"I guess I'll do the roller part. You can do all the edges and trim. You have a steady hand."

I had asked her, so I had to take the consequences. But she'd picked exactly the opposite of what I'd expected. As a perfectionist, she would have been much better at the fine details, whereas I would have been better at the roller work, which required more muscle and less attention to detail. But then I realized this would make her responsible for any roller marks that might be left. This could work out to be a very good deal.

I moved quickly to get the brushes before she changed her mind. "Okay, sounds good. I'll do the trim and you do the roller work. You know how to use a roller, right?"

"Sure." She gave a grinning salute. All the smiles were pleasant and unexpected. She was usually dead serious when we did jobs like this.

I came up with a plan about where we should start and in what order we should do things. My explanation of the plan got rather long-winded and complicated, but Linda totally accepted it. She seemed so uncharacteristically relaxed. She put on a record and began rolling, singing along with the music. The music was unfamiliar but interesting. A woman was singing about talking to Jesus, as though He were an actual person sitting right there at her kitchen table. I could see why Linda liked the songs. The woman and Linda both wanted to share what Jesus had said to them.

The painting was going quickly and smoothly. The album ended, so Linda put on Vivaldi, *The Four Seasons*. *Ah,* I thought, *some good music.* I was painting the trim on a large window. The sunlight was reflecting off the icicles hanging from the oaks and pines outside, and the music was rebounding off the walls inside. We were both humming along, and I was thoroughly enjoying the afternoon.

Vivaldi ended, and Linda put another album on. A

young woman sang with a folk guitar and occasional back-up singers. She too sang about talking to Jesus.

I glanced at Linda and was startled. For a moment she almost seemed like another person. Her body was not tense and rigid as it usually was, particularly when she focused on a job like this. She was relaxed, flowing with the music and the work. She seemed filled with joy, smiling and humming. This was not a chore to be completed but a joyous experience. She'd always been pretty, but she looked even prettier now. Her eyes caught mine. She seemed happier than I had ever seen her. I felt that this was still Linda, the same personality, but that now she could be free and happy while attending to the project. This was the real Linda, the way she was intended to be.

We had a great afternoon and finished the painting with no flaws found. As we prepared for bed that night, though, I sensed her beginning to tense up again. Later she told me that these sudden mood changes would come over her when something would remind her that I had left her before for Julie. It might be something I did or said, or it might just be a chance thought in her mind. The bedroom, with all its associations, was a common place for these "flashbacks." It brought back all the pain I had caused Linda and reopened the old wounds.

"You think I should just forget everything you've done to me," she said.

I sensed an argument coming on and tried to end it before it began. "I'm not saying that. But you can trust me now. I've changed."

"Because you say so? You're a liar. I can't trust you."

"I don't want to hear this again," I said in a dismissive tone. I was still trying to avoid the argument. I got into bed.

Linda knelt on her side of the mattress. "You will hear this! You will hear this!"

I knew that I couldn't use physical intimidation against her. "Don't bother me tonight," I said, trying to make the statement forceful enough to work.

"Why should I trust you?" she said, her voice rising. "You lied to me again and again with your half-truths. I don't trust you. You're a liar. How can I ever trust you? You twist the truth. I will not listen to you." She took the pillow from the bed, twisting it in her hands. "You don't care. You think you can be nonchalant about what you did. But you did something awful, something terrible. And you lied about it over and over."

I couldn't stand it anymore. "Enough!" I yelled. I got up and threw on some clothes. "I can't stand this nonsense. I'm leaving."

"I knew you wanted to leave. I don't know why you're here at all."

I stormed out, slamming the door to the garage. I got in the car, put the keys in the ignition, and hesitated. I wondered if I was leaving Linda merely to manipulate her. I decided that wasn't the reason. I simply couldn't withstand her attack and had left before the situation exploded. I supposed Linda was right; I had acted nonchalant about my affair with Julie. But I really didn't know what else to do. She was absolutely right. I had lied to her many times with my clever half-truths. Our breakup had caused more pain than could be patched over in just a few months. I didn't have the strength to continue apologizing, and besides, words weren't enough. I was depleted, drained, and something wasn't working anymore.

I thought about our behavior patterns. We'd been having some great days, and the severity of Linda's outbursts was decreasing. We'd stopped physically threatening each other. Those were hopeful signs. I knew I was married to Linda and any thoughts of leaving her had been eradicated by God's voice and by my own determination to stand firmly in His will. That decision was done, permanent, not changeable under any circumstances. That felt good. It was written not in sand, but in rock. It was my foundation. I was married.

But whom was I married to? As soon as I moved from analyzing myself to analyzing Linda, I became stressed and upset. If she loved God so much, why couldn't she just forgive me? That line of thought was too frustrating, so I returned to examining myself, focusing on my own contriteness and

God's forgiveness. I sensed my solid foundation, my peace. That was where I should concentrate.

I felt tired and wanted to go to bed. I got out of the car, went back inside, undressed, and slipped into bed. A few months ago I would have slept out in my car, gone out for breakfast, and then come home when I felt like it, letting her worry and suffer. But now I felt no malice and no need to "win." I was empty, tired, and wanted to go to sleep in our bed.

I had a wonderful deep sleep. When I awoke, Linda was already up. I found her in the kitchen, her mood unimproved.

"So you think you can walk out whenever you want," she said. "You think I care if you leave? I wish you would leave. It would be a weight off my back."

"I wasn't leaving you," I said, pouring myself a cup of coffee and trying to remain calm. "I couldn't take the argument. I left before we blew up."

"What do you mean, *we*? You mean *you* were going to explode again. So you were going to threaten me again. I wish you would leave. You're a liar."

"Listen, why don't you relax and go to work?"

"What? Don't you dare tell me what to do."

"It's just a suggestion," I said, backing away. I avoided the trap of trying to defend myself and prove that I could be trusted. The heat of the conversation dissipated, and she prepared for work. Just before leaving, she said, "I don't trust you. I trust God. He's the only reason I'm still around."

That left me alone in the kitchen with a lot of frustration. I paced back and forth in the narrow room, making scrambled eggs and complaining to God.

"You told me to marry her. You said, 'You're married to Linda.' But she's impossible. I can't take her outbursts."

No answer. Yet I felt His presence, filling up the small room, almost pushing me out.

"I can't stand her attacks. This is impossible. You're the one who put us together. You can't expect me to take this nonsense. She just attacks me for no reason." I was angry, yet I knew that I was supposed to forgive her. The knowledge was there, a stark reality radiated by the presence all around me. But I was resistant.

"You can't make me forgive her. I'll never forgive her for what she's done. This is like torture. I've had enough. You don't know what it's like!"

A quiet voice whispered, "*Forgive her.*"

I scrambled the eggs furiously. "What? Forgive her? I knew it. No way." I threw down the spoon. "You want me to forgive her?" I looked up, and Jesus' face was suddenly before me. The eggs, the stove, the kitchen all faded away in the intensity of His presence. I was still angry, but I was riveted by His face, the kindness in His eyes. When I had seen Him earlier in the clouds, He had been majestic and beautiful. Although his compassion had touched me, he was more distant than now. This time He seemed almost humble, and I felt a stronger, closer personal connection to Him. It was as if He was standing right in front of me. I felt myself leaning toward Him, drawn closer.

"Forgive her," Jesus said, in that same voice in which He had told me earlier that I was married to Linda.

His words were a command that contained an entreaty. I sensed hope within them, the possibility of a solution to our problem.

As much as I was captivated by Him, I was still angry. "You don't understand how she treats me," I said. "I can't forgive her."

His lips rose in a kind, fully comprehending smile. "I do understand. My enemies nailed Me to a cross and crucified Me." There was a short pause. "I forgave them."

I stumbled back in surrender. My anger vanished in a rush of compassion, and in that moment my heart opened to the presence of God. I had asked Him before to come into me, but I hadn't been ready. Now I was. Jesus had not dominated or controlled, but waited patiently until the right time, then walked right in. I felt a tremendous sense of peace and forgiveness. This was much deeper than what I'd felt the first time. It filled my being. Jesus had gone far beyond proving to me that He worked. I felt an overwhelming love for Him. And from Him I sensed love and unconditional acceptance. The spark of longing that I had experienced was ignited into a flame inside of me. Tears ran down my face.

"Vinnie," He said, "I want you to know that I took all the pain and torment for you even when you were opposed to Me. Linda is not your enemy, and she is not opposed to you. She is very hurt, more than you are. I want you to change your perception of her. She's in severe pain. I want you to see beyond the pain. Forgive her totally and it will make you free. I will give you the ability to do it." I felt the pain I had caused her and tried to process the emotions that I knew she was feeling.

I was so anxious to receive guidance that I quickly asked for more. "What am I supposed to do? How am I supposed to help her?" My request for guidance, combined with contriteness of spirit, and a sincere desire to do what He said drew a response from God.

He repeated patiently, "Forgive her."

"Okay, yes. But what do I do if she explodes again?"

"Let her be. I'm going to heal her."

"Wow, okay. You mean I don't have to do anything."

"Yes, you do. Forgive her, see her as I see her, and accept her as she is."

"I will. I will." Joy began to bubble up from the peace inside me. His words produced a sense of liberty and freedom. I was not responsible for healing Linda. I was not responsible for making Linda happy. Only God could do those things. I had only to cooperate with Him and contribute whatever positive influence I could. My responsibility was to forgive, to perceive her pain and see beyond it, to totally accept her. I got it. He was telling me to be like Him, not controlling or manipulative in any way. No control, no analysis, no manipulation, no explanation, no convincing—just absolute forgiveness.

Jesus' face had faded away, the kitchen was around me once again. I quickly pushed the overcooked eggs off the burner, not wanting to lose my train of thought. Jesus had filled my heart. I realized that this was a turning point for me. There was no going back; I completely trusted Him. He gave unconditionally, expecting nothing in return. And I was compelled to do the same. I suddenly realized why Linda had been so angry earlier this morning. She had probably been afraid last night when I stormed out that I was going to leave her. I was able to feel her pain and see beyond it. She was hurt and I needed to earn her trust, not by talking about it, but by fully forgiving and unconditionally loving. Then she would trust me. It seemed simple.

There might be some time delay between my forgiveness and the development of trust. That was just the way God had worked with me. He stayed with me and forgave and forgave until I trusted Him enough to let Him walk into my heart. So I had to stay with Linda and forgive and forgive until she let me walk back into her heart.

And He had given me the ability to forgive her with the power of His word. My old ways needed to die and be replaced by this new way. I chose to switch from self-defense and selfishness to a magnificent offense of unconditional love. I desired to stand in His forgiveness and persist.

I tried to see Linda as Jesus did, and in my mind a vivid picture arose of her heart. The surface was an irregular, hardened mass of scar tissue and scabs. Injuries had been encapsulated and preserved, unable to be released. Inside, it was dark, black, and empty. Very little could penetrate the scar tissue on the outside. I went further in, to the chamber where she kept her love for me. It was blue, bruised, and diseased.

Then an image of a different heart appeared. It was filled with the light of God. Although a few minor wounds marred the surface, the heart muscle was soft, pliable, and translucent, with no permanent scars, no encapsulations. The chamber where she kept her love for me had changed from a bruised blue to a healthy red, but it was empty, and its soft lining was filled with sensitive nerve endings. I realized that a transfusion had taken place. The blood of Jesus, admitted into the innermost chambers to mingle with Linda's, had purified, cleansed, and healed her heart. Jesus was healing her. I wasn't so glad that the chamber for me was vacant, but I sensed that for a genuine healing it had to be empty before it could be filled. I needed patience.

I shook myself out of the imagery and turned off the stove burner. As I scraped the overdone eggs into the garbage, I smiled and was astonished over that fact that I'd actually had a conversation with Jesus right there in the kitchen. Just like the woman on the record. I glanced around the room for a few minutes in stunned amazement. It was the first time in a long time that I'd been truly happy. Happiness came with His voice. Peace and unconditional love came with His voice. Hope and a plan for the future came with His voice. I was riding the highest high I'd ever felt. I was in a state of ecstasy.

While His simple assertion that I was married to Linda had helped clarify my determination to make the marriage work, I hadn't known how to make that happen until now. Now I had a plan.

I thought of Linda's wounded heart and compassion welled up inside me. It seemed easier to forgive her. "I forgive you," I said, and it felt as if it was done, though I still had to tell her.

I thought of what Jesus had said, to forgive no matter what. I repeated the word. "*Forgive.* I'm going to forgive." But I knew that if Linda began attacking me, it might be difficult to keep these good thoughts, difficult to remember to accept her totally, difficult to stand in forgiveness. "No matter what, forgive," I said to myself. "No matter what. I'm going to make a stand. I choose to forgive. Jesus is helping me to forgive. No matter what, I will forgive."

I started to do the breakfast dishes, still thinking this through. "It's settled. I've decided ahead of time. It's done.

I forgive no matter what happens." I was fixing my will to do what Jesus had said. I planted the word deep down in my heart.

"I have to let her be. Let her be." Jesus was healing her. That wasn't my job. I just had to accept her as she was.

The more I meditated on Jesus' words, the simpler things became. I was amazed, because this was contrary to my usual process. Typically, the more I dwelled on something, the more complicated it became. But with Jesus, things resolved themselves with crisp simplicity. I had to cherish His words and hold on to them at all costs. I thought to myself, *This works. There's nothing else like it.*

SEVEN

STANDING IN HIS WORD

T he day went by quickly in prayer, meditation, and joy. Soon I found myself in the kitchen again, preparing a special dinner for Linda. I was singing and dancing as I worked, in an almost giddy state. I couldn't wait to tell Linda that I forgave her. But then I wondered for a moment exactly what I was forgiving her for. Jesus seemed sort of all-inclusive when He forgave. I guessed I was forgiving her for everything, but foremost for all the aggravation she'd put me through over the last few months. But it didn't seem right to point to Linda as the source of all aggravation. That didn't seem to be the acceptance Jesus had been talking about. He didn't view her as a source of aggravation. I realized I had a little refining to do before I talked to Linda and made a mental note to work on it once I had the dinner under control.

Ecstatic, I cooked, danced, and sang. On the stereo, I played the record where the woman sang about talking to Jesus. The songs made sense to me now. I understood.

I began to make a salad. In the past, I would either have begrudgingly made the salad exactly as Linda would have made it to avoid conflict, resenting her all the while; or I would have made it exactly the way I wanted, knowing she wouldn't like it. Yet the salad I was making now was neither of these. Without thinking, I was incorporating ingredients that both of us liked, while leaving out those that one of us didn't like. I liked carrots in my salad, and tossed in big chunks when I was feeling defiant. Linda chopped everything up small and hated big chunks of any kind. On the cutting board before me, I found I'd cut the carrots into thin slices without even thinking. I realized I was applying Jesus' words to the mundane tasks of making a salad. His words had so permeated my being that they were being acted upon even in this simple way. I was no longer motivated by my desperation to make Linda happy so that I could be happy; and I was no longer feeling such anger that I wanted to spite her. I was simply happy, and I wanted to share some of my happiness. I hoped that she would enjoy the salad, but whether or not she enjoyed it was really up to her.

I put the salad on the dining room table and lit two cream-colored, hand-dipped candles I'd found tucked away in the antique cabinet that sat in the corner. Everything looked perfect.

I caught the reflection of Linda's headlights in the window and ran to meet her. I flung open the door to the garage as she was getting out of the car.

"Hi," I said. "How was your day? I'm glad you're home."

Linda replied cautiously. "Hi. How are you?"

"Great, great. Come on in. I want to show you something." She didn't even have time to put down the mail as I rushed her through the kitchen and into the dining room.

"It's nice," she said. "It's nice. Those are the candlesticks I was saving for next Thanksgiving."

"I'll buy you more candlesticks," I said, my joy and enthusiasm bubbling over. "I'll buy you whatever candlesticks you want. I'll take you to the store myself, and we'll get all the candles you want."

She stared at the salad for a few seconds, then turned to me, her expression neutral. She still had her jacket on, the mail in her hand. I could tell she wanted to go back to her normal coming-home routine. But I didn't want her to.

"I have something important to tell you," I said.

"What is it?"

I touched her arm and looked directly into her hazel eyes, thinking how much I loved her. "I forgive you." My face broke out in a huge smile.

Linda jerked away from my touch. "You what? You *what?*"

Her tone was incredulous. "*You* forgive *me*! Where do you get off forgiving me? I didn't do anything to you. You're crazy. You forgive me. It's me that has to forgive you for what you did!"

I extended my hands, joy still bubbling out of me. "Oh, come on, baby. Give me a little hug. I forgive you."

Her disbelief was fading into anger. "You think this is funny? This is not funny. You're not funny."

I realized that I was close to ruining everything. Although my first instinct, developed over many years, was to subtly shift the blame onto her, I forced myself to take responsibility. "I understand that your heart has been wounded, that you have a section of raw, exposed nerves. I know that I caused it. I hurt you."

"That's right," Linda said. "You sure did."

"I did, and I'm sorry. But I can't heal you. Jesus is going to heal you."

Linda and I stared into each other's eyes, and I felt as if I could see right into her soul, could see the words making contact, penetrating. The lines in her face softened, and I could see that she accepted the truth of the words. We stood a moment in silence.

I returned to the kitchen to complete the preparations for dinner. She put the mail down, took her jacket off, and came in to help. We got the food out onto the table and sat down together, just the two of us since Jason was at a friend's house. Linda's mood seemed peaceful, and as we ate and talked, she actually began to smile. I told her that I'd talked to Jesus in the kitchen, just like on the records she had, and that He was helping me. She seemed happy for me. I told her how I'd overcooked the eggs while I was talking to Him, and she laughed, her eyes crinkling and her whole face lighting up. I couldn't remember the last time I'd seen her laugh.

Midway through the dinner, Linda said, "The salad is delicious."

I smiled and thought to myself, *This Jesus is real.*

We got through the evening and up to bed with no sign of trouble. We lay in bed, bodies touching, Linda reading a magazine and I the Bible, which seemed ever more readable and coherent. Yet suddenly she began to question me about Julie, her anger quickly accelerating. I slid away on the bed, unable to believe the same old cycle was starting after we'd had such a great breakthrough. But this time, as my own emotions began to build toward anger, I thought of the image I had seen of Linda's heart. The raw nerves were flaring up. I had to experience her feelings, stand in forgiveness, and not follow my old patterns.

"I'm very sorry for what I did to you," I said.

But her pain was too great to be so easily soothed, and she continued, her voice growing louder, her hands moving more emphatically.

I reached over to comfort her and she flinched away. I realized then what little control she had over this whole sequence of behavior. Going to bed triggered thoughts of me with Julie, which then revived her pain and anger. I forced myself to stop my analysis. My job was not to analyze Linda. It was to accept and forgive. I allowed my mind to go quiet, and inside a soft voice said, "Leave us. I'm going to heal her."

I sat up. "Linda! Jesus is going to heal you."

Linda was startled, but still angry. "What? What do you know about Jesus? You're a liar."

I stood. I had to let her be. I would go watch *Monday Night Football.* "Linda, Jesus is going to heal you. I'll see you in a little while. I'm going downstairs to watch football." And I went downstairs.

This was very unlike me. Normally I would have argued with her until things reached a critical point. Or I would have pretended to go to sleep. I turned on the TV and sat down, feeling very strange. I hadn't watched football in years, though I'd played it in college and loved it. I hadn't watched it because Linda didn't like it, and I'd always been concerned with making her happy. I felt that this was the real me. I was more alive in this moment than I'd been in a long time.

The game was the Cowboys versus the Giants, a great contest. At half-time I reflected on what had happened with

Linda and whether or not it would work. She appeared to be in more pain now than she'd ever been. It didn't seem like there would be any end to it.

"What's going on here?" I implored Jesus with a pressing determination.

"I'm healing her," He said.

"But it doesn't look like she's being healed."

His voice was calm, reassuring. "There's often a time delay between receiving the truth into the heart and the outward manifestation of that truth. You may not fully understand now that Linda can be in severe pain, and you may still feel anger toward her and argue with her. I can short-circuit the time factor and bring an immediate, complete healing. However, I want to teach you both a few things and develop your character. Therefore your healing will be progressive."

"Oh, yes, yes," I said. His words encouraged me to continue standing.

"Her heart contains good soil," He said. "She has the heart of David. It will not be long before the seedlings of My word sprout forth with new life."

"Yes," I said, though I wasn't sure what He meant.

"Go upstairs and take a look at how she's doing," He said.

I went upstairs. Linda was sleeping, her face smooth and relaxed, her breathing deep and peaceful. I somehow sensed the healing going on inside her, like a warmth she radiated.

I hurried back downstairs to catch the second half, but

after a minute or two of viewing, I turned off the TV, went back upstairs, and got into bed beside Linda. I thought to myself, *Wow, this works. This Jesus really works. He was right there, at the half-time. What He said was clear, easy, right. I'm free. Thank God, I'm free.*

I felt as though I could fly right through the ceiling and glide through the sky. I remembered the dreams I'd had as a child, when I flew like an eagle over farmlands and forests. I'd regained the ability to fly, my spirit soaring into the heavens to give thanks to God. I rolled over toward Linda, gently put my arm around her, and drifted off into a sweet, restful sleep.

EIGHT

DIGGING DEEPER

The next morning, as soon as Jason and Linda had left, I took the Bible and went over to the couch to sit and listen to God. Now that I had heard His voice so clearly, I didn't want to stop. It had become my habit to read the Bible for an hour or more, and then to reflect on what I'd read. But this morning I was too excited to stay with the reading. I was proud of the way I'd handled things last night, and a bit full of myself. I put the Bible down and closed my eyes.

I tried to draw Jesus into a casual conversation. I said, "I did pretty good, didn't I?"

There was no answer.

I thought of the images I had seen of Linda's heart, how wounded it was with its scabs and encapsulations. She was really a wreck. It would even take Jesus a while to heal her.

"Stop," a gentle voice said. "Don't judge her. Judge yourself."

I was glad that the voice had returned. I had come to realize that listening, understanding, and then acting on Jesus' words brought significant, dramatic results. So I wanted to understand. I remembered my previous impression, that a sincere request for guidance combined with contriteness of spirit drew a response from God. I hungered for more.

"Was I judging her?" I asked.

"Yes, you were critically examining her heart. I showed you her heart so that you could understand and have compassion for her, not so that you would judge her. Do not judge her. Forgive her." I perceived in my spirit that my freedom and liberty depended on a solid understanding of this point.

"Yes." I pressed on. "Does my freedom depend on this?"

"If you judge, then you will be judged, and you will walk under the law. But if you forgive, you will be forgiven, and you will walk under My grace."

That made immediate sense to me. "I see."

"It's like a pendulum. Whenever you judge, judgment will come back to you. Whenever you forgive, forgiveness will come back to you. Which pendulum would you like to be on?"

"Forgiveness. Definitely forgiveness. But how do I do it?"

"Just do it."

I remembered how Jesus had forgiven me, the great weight that had been lifted from me. I sensed that, in receiving His forgiveness, I had also gained the ability to forgive. But although it had seemed so simple, it was difficult to do. I was honest with Him. "It's hard."

He said firmly, "Judge yourself and forgive her."

I noticed that when He was on a certain subject He tended to stay with it. The conversation had come full circle. While there were peace and joy in His words, there was also a sense of gravity. I knew that His message was critically important to me. I had been operating totally opposite to God's way. My tendency had been to evaluate, judge, and blame someone else, perhaps not directly but subtly, while thinking pretty highly of myself. I needed to kill that tendency, to replace it with God's way, to judge myself and forgive Linda. I needed help.

"Jesus, help me. Show me how to do it."

"Examine yourself in the light of the word that I have given you. You are responsible for keeping the word that I have given you. If you fall short, humble yourself and ask for My help. I will cleanse you. But remember that you are responsible for keeping the word that I have given you."

"Thank You. That's very clear. I understand." I nodded agreement, yet I pondered, *But didn't I forgive Linda? I thought I forgave her.* I wasn't doubting Him. I was questioning for a full understanding.

He said, "You made the decision to forgive her and planted My word in your heart. But you have some weeds among the good seeds."

As much as I would have liked to deny this, I knew that I did still harbor some resentment toward Linda. It seemed impossible to get rid of. "Show me. Help me." I pleaded.

"Your heart has decayed areas of infection and pollution, which have sprung up out of roots of bitterness you have allowed to take hold. Bitterness toward Linda."

His words frightened me, but there was no place else to go. He held the words, the solutions, and the ability. I had to follow. I looked into my heart and saw the bitterness over past incidents: over my inability to please her; over the love for her horse, which had seemed greater than her love for me; over her perfectionism, which dictated that nothing I did was good enough. The list of offenses was endless, the bitter roots everywhere.

"What do I do? How do I get them out?"

"Give them to me," Jesus said. "Give them all to me, and I will replace them with love and kindness."

My heart had broken like a fragile vase, but it still carried so much bitterness inside. I opened up my heart to Him and let it all go. A dark cloud rose out of my heart, dense and filled with offenses, slights cherished and held close. A great sense of lightness and sweetness filled my heart. It was a very gentle process. I felt cleansed by His word and His presence. And with His presence, an inseparable part of it, came His kindness. I had felt His kindness and sensed my own lack in this area, wanting to be more like Him. Now I felt something within myself set free: the ability to be kind, to love. Moreover, the joy of a childlike honesty, tempered with a sober sense of integrity and truthfulness, pervaded my consciousness. I bowed my head in grateful acknowledgment of the goodness of God.

NINE

FINDING EACH OTHER

I discovered that hard work was involved in order to continue to diligently seek God. Some days were spent in silence, ending with exhaustion over my spent efforts. On occasional gray afternoons when the ground outside had thawed, I ventured into the yard for some rugged exercise under massive bare oaks. I dug up and transplanted some huge bushes and small trees. I wrestled with rhododendrons, mountain laurels, azaleas, white pines, and hemlocks, as I struggled with thoughts over past failures and mistakes. Nevertheless, my habit to read the Bible for an hour or so had expanded to hours on end, often accompanied by continual reflection and tenacious prayer. I frequently lost track of time, enfolded in an overall sense of delight in God with the exhilaration of an adventure that surely I would find some hidden treasure under the next stone that had to be rolled away. Winter was passing. A glorious spring and summer were on the horizon. I was finding God and finding Linda as well.

It was amazing how quickly I progressed with my determined plan to forgive Linda, to see her in the way that God saw her, to accept her completely, and to let her be. It was especially incredible when I considered how long I had been doing exactly the opposite: seven years. And those patterns had formed long before I had even met Linda. But with God's help I was learning to change. I had found that despite what I'd thought, I'd never really accepted Linda. My acceptance had been a cloak hiding a series of judgments and accusations.

I felt that my healing was moving along rapidly, and I was excited to put into practice new ways and principles. I wanted to express to others the kindness and goodness God had imparted to me. Although occasional flare-ups with Linda still occurred, they were less frequent and less violent. She was beginning to understand that I wasn't going to leave her no matter what, and she was slowly starting to trust me again. It seemed to me now a good thing that God's healing was gradual. The process was gentler this way and allowed us both time to sift through our feelings. God had told me that He wanted to teach us a few things in the process, and I focused on what those things might be.

I realized that while I could sense God's kindness flowing

within me, it would be some time before the internal change would be consistently reflected in my external actions. Before I could give away love, or kindness, or peace, it had to be an integral part of me. While God had touched my spirit and my heart with His kindness, my mind still had to incorporate this change. I had a lot of old habits to discard and new habits to form. They didn't come easily or automatically. And kindness was only one of the characteristics of Jesus that I wanted to emulate. The whole process would take time.

But I wanted to share what Jesus had given me with others. I knew that whatever I gave, I would receive, but I also knew there could be a time delay between giving and receiving. I shouldn't expect too much too soon. I had given Linda unconditional love and sensed it would be some time before she could return it. Yet, if I was truly, completely transformed, then I should be able to maintain that characteristic, that unconditional love, no matter how long the time delay. I was still working on that part. I needed to try to act on this kindness, and to stand in kindness no matter how the other person responded.

It all made perfect sense, but in order to do this, I needed God's grace. This carried me back to the beginning. I had to be humble and acknowledge my need for His help in order to live well and become more like Jesus. I didn't have the ability to express peace, or love, or kindness, or joy in all situations. I needed God's divine influence.

I chose to practice on Linda. That day I would give freely to Linda whatever I had received from God, with no strings attached. That was the bottom line: to give and give. And I had to give without getting caught up in my old trap of needing to make her happy. I saw four things that I needed to do, that I hadn't really done in a long time if ever—the four things that God had done for me. I had to give. I had to stop finding fault and blame, and instead of tearing Linda down, to help build her up and strengthen her. Her heart was wounded and needed strength. I needed to communicate, to share, talk, and listen to Linda as concertedly as I did with God. That was something I had never done. And I had to touch her, as God had touched me, to make an emotional connection.

I understood that after God, who came first, Linda was my top priority. Every day I made a decision to give, to build her up, to communicate, and to make contact with her, connect with her. I would need help from God to do it, but I was firm in my purpose.

I thought about how Linda liked beautiful flowers, and this led me to think about how picky she was. But maybe it wasn't pickiness. Maybe she appreciated excellence and sought it out. Perhaps this tendency was a gift rather than a drawback. Yet many times it seemed to bring her unhappiness. If she wanted to buy a dress, it had to be the perfect dress. She had difficulty deciding which one was the most perfect; so much seemed to ride on the choice. I saw that below the shell of assertiveness lurked fear and indecisiveness. She was her own worst critic, never satisfied with anything she did. And I sensed that underlying this dissatisfaction was the fear that, if she were less than perfect, she would be discovered and rejected—by me, her family, friends, everyone—and her life would spiral out of control. My leaving her must have been one of the worst things that could have happened to her.

I thanked Jesus for healing her. I accepted Linda as she was and loved her. And I prayed for her, knowing that one day the fear would be cast away and she would become whole.

At about four in the afternoon Linda came home and was surprised by the flowers on the cutting board in the kitchen. I had given her flowers in the past only on special occasions.

"Oh, how beautiful," she exclaimed. "I love fresh flowers."

I came up behind her and grabbed her with a brisk hug.

She started and pulled away. "Don't grab me like that. I hate it when you grab me and pull my clothes."

I was taken aback by her reaction. I let go and faced her. "I'm sorry. I just wanted to give you a little hug." I took her gently in my arms and held her for a few seconds.

She was more relaxed this time, but still pushed away. "Not now. Jason will be home soon."

"Not now? What do you mean?" I was perplexed. "I thought you liked to be held. When I want to go to sleep at night, you always say you want to be held. I'm just trying to hold you."

"I do like to be held. But not now. I don't want to be held now."

I coached myself internally to listen and understand. "Do you think whenever I touch you that I want to have sex?"

"That's true, isn't it?"

A year ago I would have been offended, judged her negatively, and then walked off. But now I was trying to listen, not to judge, to be more like Jesus. I was aware that she was right. That usually was my motive in touching her. I was judging myself, rather than Linda. It was surprising to notice how little I had touched Linda when sex wasn't on my mind. I was trying to change, to give, but Linda had no way of knowing this. And Linda liked the familiar, the routine. There might be a time delay before she was ready to receive this change.

"I don't want to go to bed," I said. "I just want to hold you for a few seconds. Okay?"

She seemed slightly annoyed, anxious over the change in me. "Well, okay," she said.

As I held her gently, a small voice within my spirit said, "Now why don't you try that again tonight, when she prefers to be held and you will be slightly inconvenienced."

I replied silently, "Yes. That's right."

Linda stepped away and began to look through the mail.

"I want to thank you for being so faithful," I said. "I know that you're a very committed person and you stuck by me even when I was way out of line."

Linda put the mail down. "I'm not committed to you. God told me that if He brought you back home then you would be better and stay for good this time. I'm committed to God. I believe Him. I trust Him."

The phone rang and Linda went to take the call in the hallway. *Well,* I thought, *at least she liked the flowers.*

"What!" Linda cried out.

I went into the hall, where she clenched the phone to her ear.

"Oh no. He couldn't have . . . When . . . Where did it happen? . . . Was anyone hurt?"

I stood beside Linda as she hung up the phone. Her voice was a monotone. "Jason is at the police station. He and his friend Omar have been arrested for shooting out the windows of some school buses with a BB gun." She hesitated, then said the rest in a rush. "A driver was in one of the buses when they shot at it. They could have shot him."

I took Linda's hand. "Was anyone injured?"

"No. No one was physically hurt. But the man was terrified. The driver was an older man, retired. Can you imagine that poor old man driving the bus with those kids shooting at the windows? I can't imagine what they could have been thinking. How could they have done this?"

I shook my head. "Who was on the phone?"

"Someone from the school district. I don't even remember his name. He sounded disgusted with Jason. How could we have let him do this? He's our responsibility."

"Jason is the one who's going to have to take responsibility for his choices. Let's go."

Linda grabbed her jacket and joined me in the car. "Jason is going to have to take responsibility and so are you. I told you not to give him that BB gun."

We drove in silence to the station. I still felt at peace, yet a few doubts had begun to surface. This wasn't the first time Linda had "told me so" when it came to Jason. I tended to give him more freedom, even if it meant he would make a mistake. Linda didn't want Jason to make any mistakes, to get hurt. She wanted to protect him from all that. I wondered whether I had made a mistake in letting him have the BB gun. It certainly seemed so. Yet guns were neutral. They could be used by a variety of people for a variety of purposes. I had thought Jason could handle the responsibility. I wanted to get God's perspective on this.

We rushed into the police station and found the officer who had taken Jason into custody. He pointed us toward a small room where Jason was waiting, where we could talk to him. Omar's mother had already arrived and was talking to Omar in a separate room. I knew she was very strict, and I expected Omar was getting some strong consequences for his inappropriate behavior. When we entered the room, Jason jumped up from his seat, looking relieved to see us. "Boy, am I glad you came," he said.

Linda put her hands on her hips. "Do you have any idea what you've done?"

Jason looked down. "We were walking down Burrs Lane and shooting at some targets—cans and rocks mostly—that we saw. When we came up past the bus lot we had just shot a few empty soda bottles and watched the glass break. We didn't plan to shoot at the windows. It just happened."

Linda took his chin and lifted his face to hers. "Those windows didn't shoot themselves out."

"No, we did it. I took some shots, and Omar did too."

"And did he shoot at the bus with the driver?" Linda asked.

Jason looked away. "Well, no, that was me."

Linda let go of her anger and pleaded. "Oh, Jason, what could you have been thinking? You could have blinded the man. An older retired man was driving the bus. You scared him terribly."

"I'm sorry, Mom. I didn't think about scaring the man. I knew the gun wasn't strong enough to shatter the windows. We just broke the bottles at close range. We were shooting at these parked buses and then I saw one moving, a moving target, and I couldn't resist. It was sort of like a challenge. I was showing off. I'm sorry. I didn't mean to hurt or scare the man."

Linda's tone grew more gentle. "Just think about it. Suppose he was your grandfather. Would you like it if someone shot at your grandfather?"

"No, I wouldn't," Jason replied.

Linda nodded.

Jason looked over at me. "I had to fill out some forms. I think you need to sign them. I got most of it, but I didn't know what to put for religion since my father was Catholic and my mother is Jewish."

"What did you put down?" I asked.

"I put down that I believe in God," he said. "I prayed to God to get me out of this mess. That's why I was so glad to see you and Mom when you came in."

"God is going to get you out of this mess," I said, glad that he had asked God for help. "And you are going to pay for any damage that was done and apologize to the driver. The officer has told us that we will have to appear in family court to face charges made against you by the school district."

Jason was released and we headed back home. I grasped the apparent fact that Jason had not been old enough or responsible enough to have a gun. I had made a mistake. I saw that in my constant battles with Linda over Jason, I would automatically take the permissive side, judging her to be overprotective and wrong no matter what the issue. I hadn't really thought about whether the BB gun would be good for Jason. I had simply made the decision out of habit, judging my way to be superior. I had to correct this error and pay more attention to Jason and his needs.

We were all concerned with the driver and his condition, and we decided that when we got home we would call the school district, ask to meet with the driver, and offer apologies and any assistance. We pulled into the driveway, and Linda went in to make the call.

I told Jason to stay in the garage with me. The police had returned the BB gun to us, and now I took it out of the bag. "Jason, I'm going to destroy this gun and throw it away." I dismantled the gun in front of him, breaking some of the mechanisms so it couldn't be put back together. I threw the pieces into the garbage. "I'm not totally against guns, but I don't think that, with the way things have gone, we should hold the gun as a privilege that you can earn back. You went over the line, and you're not going to be using a gun for a very long time."

Jason didn't dispute the decision. He was glad to be home and out of the mess, at least for a while. We went inside, finding Linda hanging up the hall phone.

"Fortunately the driver is okay," she said. "He doesn't want to meet with us. He says he was startled at the time, but he's okay now. He accepts your apology and doesn't feel it's necessary to get together."

Jason was more relieved than she was, and he went up to his room to lie down.

I told Linda that I had destroyed the gun and that she was right, Jason hadn't been ready for it. I asked her if she would mind if I spent some time alone so I could find out if God had anything to say about this. She left me alone in the living room. I felt it was critical to seek God's point of view on Jason's behavior and our own responses. I reviewed the events. At first I was too preoccupied by everything that had happened, but after a few minutes I was able to quickly sink into the rest and presence of God. I understood that my practice of entering into God's presence every morning made it easier to do so now, in the aftermath of a crisis. I began to feel compassion for Jason and a need to apologize to him. I questioned in my spirit whether he had a serious problem. I didn't think so. He didn't seem angry. Rather, his life was not structured enough; it lacked a clear direction. I started to evaluate myself in relation to him, as I had learned to evaluate myself in relation to Linda. I had been physically absent for periods over the past year, but I had been emotionally absent for a much longer time that continued up to the present. It was not a pleasant realization. I examined myself further and was relieved to see that I held no resentments, no judgments or bitterness against Jason. I felt love for Jason. But I had recently learned that God's love involved commitment and laying down one's life, even for one's enemies. Jason was my friend, and I wasn't exactly laying down my life for him. I felt guilty for my neglect, and I brought my feelings of guilt to

Jesus, who, as always, immediately forgave and released me.

God whispered, "You had to be broken and healed before you could give anything to Linda. You have progressed enough now that you can continue to give to Linda and also sow into Jason." I felt a great peace and a sense of rightness in the statements.

I asked what I was to do, and how.

Instructions came. "Apologize to him for your absence. Tell him that, although you will not permit the behavior that he showed today, you will take some of the responsibility as his father. And tell him you plan to spend more time with him."

After dinner Jason and I went down to the basement to shoot a game of pool. We had a professional style, six-foot slate base table on which we used to wage some fierce competitions, but which we hadn't used lately.

Jason banked the six ball off the side and into the corner pocket.

"Nice shot, Jason."

"Thanks," he said, considering his next shot.

"Jason, I have to apologize for leaving home and being away, and breaking some of my commitments toward you."

He let me off the hook easily. "Oh, that's okay. Seven ball in the side pocket." He lined up the shot, made it.

"I think you need some direction. I think that we should spend more time together. What would you like to do?"

Jason straightened, his eyes wide with hope and excitement. "Fishing. I'd like to go fishing. We could go to Herman's Sports and get some equipment tonight, right after we finish the game."

That was classic Jason: do it now, don't stop to think about it. I thought, *Great idea. Fishing instead of shooting.* "Let's include your mother," I suggested. "Maybe she'd like to go with us, and we can all take a fishing trip."

Linda didn't think much of fishing, especially after the shooting incident. In the past, I would have been obsessed with making her happy and would have gone along with whatever plan she wanted. But I felt that I was being led to do something Jason would like and so took the unaccustomed position of leader. My enthusiasm made me a little pushy, and I convinced Linda to go along on the trip for Jason's sake.

An hour later, Jason was racing through Herman's, going from tents to inflatable boats to fishing gear. Linda reined him in, and they compromised on rods, reels, lures, lines, a tackle box, and, after a little controversy, a decent fishing knife. I had pushed the tent idea, but both Jason and Linda thought that outdoor activities could be successfully combined with the luxuries of a modern hotel.

We returned home with our cache of supplies and agreed that we would take our trip the next weekend, which included a school holiday near the end of the semester on

Friday. I was tired and sank with satisfaction into bed, but then I remembered the words of the Spirit earlier that day. I rolled over to Linda and put my arms around her. She cuddled up, glad for the physical contact.

"Could you rub my back?" she asked.

In the past, I had resented her requests for back rubs, which I fulfilled grudgingly. Whenever I would stop, she'd always want more, which left me feeling like a failure. But this time I felt no resentment, because it had been my idea to initiate the touch and because I realized how important it was. I slid one of my arms from around her and began to rub her back, starting at the neck and working my way down. As I continued, I felt her body relax, and finally she drifted into sleep. I mused that this was probably the first time Linda felt truly comfortable in our bed since our troubles had first begun.

TEN

SPRING

I made arrangements to rent a cabin for the weekend on the shore of the Great Sacandaga Lake in upstate New York. Taking into consideration both Linda and Jason's desire for luxury and my own for a tent, I compromised in picking a simple cabin with electricity and a hot plate. We left early Friday morning and arrived a few hours later, filled with anticipation and excitement.

We climbed out of the car and I took in the view. Just across the road, the lake was huge, shining in the sun and surrounded by trees. Behind us, the little cabin looked cute, tucked into a patch of woods. The trees were a spring shade of light green. Beyond them rose the mountains, perfect for hiking.

"Well, look at that view," I said, stretching my arms. I took in a deep breath of fresh air. "This is great."

"What's that little building next to the cabin?" Jason asked.

"That's the outhouse," Linda replied. "Right next to the one-room shack."

I refused to let Linda's tone dampen my enthusiasm, though I acknowledged I hadn't asked if the place had a bathroom. We pulled our suitcases and equipment out of the car, and I crossed my fingers as we entered the cabin. The place looked as if it had been furnished circa 1960, the couch threadbare, the curtains dark and dingy. Instantly the complaints began. Linda couldn't believe there was only one double bed and no shower, and Jason was amazed to find there was no television, no stereo, no radio.

"There's no TV," he said for the third time. "There's no phone. Can you believe there's no phone? What if we have to make a call?"

"We don't need a TV," I said. "If we have to make a call we can go up to the main house where we got the key and make a call."

"What about the bed?" Linda asked. "Where are we going to sleep? And look at that."

She pointed to a folding table with a double hot plate and two little ceramic terrier dogs, one black and one white.

"At least they provided us with salt and pepper shakers," I said.

Jason burst out laughing, and before we knew it Linda and I had joined in.

Linda held her stomach. "I don't know what you're laughing about," she said to Jason. "You're going to sleep on the floor."

"Oh no, I'm not," Jason said, unable to stop laughing.

We settled in after that, and Linda offered to unpack and organize while Jason and I went down to the lake. We found a wooden dock and a rowboat lying on its side next to the dock. Jason and I dropped our lines in at the end of the dock. As the minutes passed and we got no bites, Jason began to change lures and baits, determined to catch something. When a half hour had passed with no results, Jason began to eye the rowboat.

"Let's check that boat out," he said.

"I don't know, Jason," I said. "I'm not sure if it's safe, and I don't know whether the boat belongs to the cabins or not."

He set down his rod and stood. "Let's just see what shape it's in." He went over to make an inspection and called back to me, excited. "The boat is in good shape. Look—there are life jackets and everything. It must belong to the cabins. Who else would leave a boat right here, next to the dock?"

I got up, drawn in by his comments, and found myself helping him put the boat in the water. As he climbed in, I said, "Let's let your mother know what we're doing and ask her to come along for a ride. Why don't you go get her?" I thought Linda might respond to Jason's enthusiasm. Within a few minutes he had dragged her down to the boat and started to make his case.

"You're not going to get me in that thing," Linda said.

"Why not?" Jason pleaded. "It floats. Here are the life jackets. Here are the oars. It's safe."

Linda crossed her arms, considering. "Can you row? Do you know how?"

I spoke up. "I know how to row. I'll teach him."

Linda took a deep breath and let it out. "Okay. Let's go."

Holding my hand on one side and Jason's on the other, Linda climbed into the boat. It started to tip over.

"Vinnie, help me!" Linda screamed.

Jason and I held on with all our might and steadied the boat. We climbed in—carefully—and pushed off the dock. It took us about forty-five minutes, Jason and I switching off on the oars, to row our way out of the inlet to the main body of the lake. We kept moving in semicircles. A straight course seemed impossible.

By the time we got out on the lake, it was late afternoon. The sky was overcast, and there was a chill in the air.

Jason and I were sweaty and tired, but not yet totally exhausted. We cast our lines into the choppy water and let the boat drift.

After a few minutes, Linda began rubbing her arms. "It's cold out here. Are you going to be able to row back?"

"Of course we can row back," Jason and I answered in tandem.

After another five minutes, I began feeling the cold as

well. The clouds were getting darker. I felt bad that Jason hadn't even had a bite on his hook. "Those clouds look like rain," I said. "I don't think we should be caught out here in the rain."

Linda chimed in. "I'm freezing out here. Let's go back."

"Okay, Mom," Jason said. "We'll take you back."

We had drifted away from the dock, and the trip back was exhausting. As Linda climbed out, I said to Jason in a manly tone, "Do you want to go back out and try another spot?"

"Nah, I don't think so," Jason replied, likewise manly. "I have to go to the bathroom."

Linda and I went back to the cabin as Jason headed for the outhouse. I dropped the fishing equipment in a corner of the cabin.

"It's good to be out of the cold," Linda said. "I have a chill down to my bones."

The door to the cabin shot open. "I'm not going to the bathroom in there," an incredulous Jason stated. "It's disgusting. It smells. You can't expect me to go in there."

I wanted to tell him to quit complaining, but paused since I'd never been in an outhouse myself. Linda smiled. "You're either gonna go in there or you're gonna go in the woods. At least you have a roof over your head in there in case it rains."

Jason looked toward the outhouse, then back at us. "Take me up to the main house and ask if I can use the toilet," he pleaded.

"No way," Linda responded.

"Let's go outside and see what the outhouse looks like," I suggested.

Linda said, "Okay," and Jason followed hesitantly.

The smell was strong, but the place was clean and had a wide plank with a large circle cut out for the seat. We bent over, peeked in, and in the dim light saw the bottom of a deep pit covered with some white powdery substance that looked like lime to me. Linda thought that it was lye, and Jason didn't care what it was.

Linda said, "It's okay. You sit on there." She motioned toward the circular opening in the plank.

"Oh no," Jason said.

"What's the matter, Jay? Are you afraid you're going to get a splinter in your backside?" I teased. "Do you want me to stay here and help you?"

"No! No! I can do it myself." He pushed us away and shut the door.

We started walking back to the cabin. Halfway back, I wheeled around. "How are you doing, Jason? Be careful you don't fall into the pit!"

A muffled reply came from inside the outhouse. "Be quiet. Someone could hear you."

Linda and I scanned the isolated area, where not a single car had passed since we arrived, and dissolved into laughter.

We had been back in the cabin for a few minutes when a

light drizzle began. Jason returned with some ruffled feathers. "Someone could have heard you."

"Oh come on, great outdoorsman. There's no one around here for miles," Linda said.

Jason changed the subject. "I'm hungry."

"Okay, there's some bread, peanut butter, and jelly in that bag over there." Linda pointed.

"Peanut butter and jelly?" He repeated.

"Yes. You guys didn't catch any fish, did you? You're lucky that I brought the peanut butter and jelly along."

We had our dinner, two sandwiches each for Jason and myself, and a single sandwich for Linda. The rain passed and she curled up in bed with a book. Jason and I tried our hand again on the wooden dock, continuing through sunset. Finally Jason turned to me and said, "Do you think you could pray and ask God to send us some fish to catch?"

I considered the request. "Well, Jason, why don't you pray?"

"Nah, you can pray better."

"I don't know. I'm not sure if I can ask Him for fish. I think it's up to you to be positive and keep trying."

Jason sighed. "It's getting dark. I think I'll go back to the cabin."

I stayed outside for a while, enjoying the dusk. I reflected on the day and appreciated the goodness of God. Despite all the blunders that I had made, we were having a wonderful time. This time I'd been too wrapped up in taking charge and doing what I thought was best. Next time I'd make sure we had a bathroom, TV, and a motorboat. Linda was making the best of it. I knew she was going to hate not being able to take a warm shower in the morning. Jason was fine, but he would have liked to watch a movie tonight. And I knew that he would have loved to have the use of a motor boat. He loved machinery and speed. But we were free, joyful, and having a great time. I looked up into the heavens and hesitatingly asked, "God, please let Jason catch some fish. Thank You." I went back inside and the three of us squeezed into the double bed.

Linda arose first, singing and full of energy. I dragged myself up soon after, tired from my uneven sleep. Jason was enjoying an undisturbed, sound sleep. Linda cooked pancakes on the hot plates, and we made plans to take a morning hike up the side of the mountain directly across from the stream. We shook Jason out of bed, had a great breakfast, and coaxed him to come with us on the hike. Although Jason was having a good time, physical exertion was not part of his preferred activity schedule.

Halfway up the mountain, he began to complain. "This is all rocky. What's the point of all this? Where are we going anyway?"

Linda playfully commented, "What's the matter? Out of shape? Can't you climb a little hill?"

"Be quiet," he yelled back, his pent-up frustration exploding out.

After a few moments, I said, "We're going to the top so we can look out from that vantage point and see the entire lake." Although neither Jason nor Linda seemed to be enthralled by the possibility of a scenic view, I had at least provided a sensible reason to continue to the top.

We huffed on for about twenty-five minutes and reached the top. "Great idea, Vin," Linda stated in a deadpan tone.

We looked around and the tall, dense trees blocked any view beyond ten or twenty feet. As usual, Jason wanted to rush right on to the next step. "Let's go back down and get off this mountain. I want to go back."

We all made eye contact and nodded approval. I took a deep breath.

"Okay, let's go," Linda said as she hiked off, apparently enjoying the exercise. Jason and I followed.

On the last leg of the journey we sped up, running down the steep, rocky slope at breakneck speed, Jason in the lead. He stumbled over some rocks and we banged into one another, nearly all falling into the stream. We had a collective, hearty laugh, all holding on to each other.

Together, we walked back to the cabin and decided to go our separate ways for the rest of the morning. Jason went exploring upstream, Linda took the car to explore the surrounding neighborhood, and I stayed in the cabin with a pamphlet she had placed near the bed.

The pamphlet contained the beatitudes, Jesus' Sermon

on the Mount. I recalled having read them awhile ago. I read them over a number of times and noticed that several of the passages accurately described some of my experiences with God. The beginning, which at one time had made no sense to me at all, was absolutely clear. Jesus said, "Blessed are the poor in spirit, for theirs is the kingdom of heaven."

That was exactly the state I was in: humbled, broken, contrite, poor in spirit. And heaven was open to me. I was blessed, free, open to God, and He had cleansed my heart, healed me. I could see Him, talk to Him.

Jesus' words stood out in another passage: "Blessed are the pure in heart, for they shall see God." I felt as if I was striking hidden treasure and went back, reading them all over again. A third phrase struck me: "Blessed are the merciful, for they shall obtain mercy." This was the giving and receiving principle with which I had been working: give and it will come back to you. This was how I had tried to deal with Jason in our recent crisis. He had been shown the firm consequences of his actions, yet we forgave him, showing him mercy and kindness. I had received mercy from Jesus and I could give mercy out to Jason. I felt awed by the simplicity and depth of it. I thanked God for His mercy and grace that had come into our lives. The Spirit of God said to me, in a small voice in the very center of my heart, "Don't be so surprised. I will lead you and guide you into all truth."

A sharp knock at the door and Linda calling my name jolted me out of my reflection. I opened the door to find Linda, a smile of success on her face, with two large bags of groceries, one in either arm. She had half-gallons of juice and milk, eggs, bacon, fruit, snacks, and some fresh flounder. I shared in her delight over the acquisitions, although the flounder not only seemed out of place as a saltwater fish but also touched a sensitive spot of disappointment over our failed attempts to catch a single fish. I was happy over her find, and wanted to reciprocate by sharing some of the finds the Holy Spirit had guided me to in the words of her pamphlet. We unpacked the food, grabbed a couple of apples, and went for a walk down the road toward the main house. We left the door unlocked for Jason and some snacks on the table that we were sure he'd love.

Sharing our experiences, we strolled down the road past some rows of fruit trees and toward the main house. It was a large, old ramshackle place with a picnic table on the front lawn. Three women in jeans and T-shirts stood outside while a bunch of children ran around and played. I recognized one of the women as the one who had handed me the key when we arrived. We waved as we walked by, and they beckoned us over. We approached and made introductions.

"Hi, I'm Vinnie and this is my wife, Linda."

"Hello, I'm Becky," said the young woman who'd given us the key. She introduced the tall, muscular woman beside her. "This is my partner, Sue." Then she pointed to the third woman, who had short blonde hair. "And this is our other partner, Ann."

"So where are you from?" Ann asked.

Linda and Ann made some small talk, and I sat on the picnic table while Becky and Sue kept an eye on the kids. Linda asked Ann if her husband was at work.

"No," Ann said, "I'm divorced."

"We almost got divorced ourselves," Linda said, and I jerked my head up, astonished by her frankness in front of these strangers. "I know what it's like to be hurt. Vinnie left me for another woman last year, and I swore I'd never take him back. But then Jesus visited me and told me that He would bring my husband back to me for good, better than ever. God brought him back to me. And while I didn't trust him and didn't trust men, I did trust God. And finally I was able to forgive him. God gave me the ability to forgive."

My face was red, but all three women were closely paying attention to Linda, and after a moment they all began to speak.

"That's amazing," Becky said. "I—"

"Yes," Ann interrupted. "My husband is no good. He left me last year."

"Mine beat me and I left him," Sue said.

"It's amazing that you're saying these things to us," Becky said. "My husband also left me for another woman. It's like you walked right up and knew what was going on. We've all been abused in one way or another by men, so we got together and bought this place."

"I wouldn't take my husband back if he crawled on his hands and knees and begged me," Sue said.

Linda replied in a peaceful, sure tone that captured the three women. "I'm more concerned about you, the condition of your hearts, that you won't be bitter and hardened against people, particularly men, whether they come back or not. You've been through so much pain. You need to be healed. You can be healed, and with the power of God you can not only survive but become better people. Then you can trust God to lead you concerning your husbands and what you should do. You'll be healthy, strong, and able to function."

"How do we get healed?" Ann asked.

"I don't know if I want to get healed," Sue said. "I'll never trust that wife-beater again."

Linda calmly continued. "You ask Jesus to help you forgive. He will do it. He will help you forgive and He will heal you. But then—and this is important—His Spirit will lead you, guide you about your husbands. I don't think He will lead you back into an abusive situation. You see, you can trust Jesus. He won't fail you. You know, Sue, I'm not at all suggesting that you should trust your husband, especially if he abused you. I'm saying that Jesus can take away your bitterness, heal you, and let you know whether you will ever be able to trust him, or for that matter whether or not you can expect him to come back."

Sue stiffened. "I told you that I don't want him back, period, whether I'm healed or not."

Linda reached her hand toward Sue. They made brief physical contact with a squeeze of their hands. Linda shared. "I don't want to intrude on your personal life, Sue. I just care about you, that's all."

Sue returned a soft smile. She replied. "Thanks, I can feel your concern." Their hands made contact again with a firmer grasp as they made a strong, momentary connection.

"I know that I need to be able to forgive my husband," Becky said. "Thank you. Thank you. What brought you up here anyway?"

Linda gave a small laugh. "I'm just up here on this fishing trip for my son. Oh"—she turned to me—"I wonder how Jason is? We better get back."

We shared several hugs with the women and started back to the cabin. I was amazed at what had happened. I felt that Linda had really helped those women, had sowed seeds that perhaps in the future would take root. "How did you know what to say? How did you know what was happening there?"

Linda shrugged. "I don't know. I just picked up in my spirit that they had been hurt, were hurting, and I opened my mouth to share what God had done for me."

As we approached the cabin, we saw Jason on the dock, fishing. We saluted, he waved back, and we went in to prepare dinner. I sat down and let Linda do the cooking. She was pleased with the afternoon and hummed a tune as she whipped up a batter for the flounder and began to fry it.

Jason burst in with a five-inch fish dangling from the end of his line. "Look what I caught! Look what I caught!"

I jumped out of my seat and patted him on the back. Linda marveled over it. "Wow! That's wonderful."

After a few moments he looked over and saw the fish in the pan. He thought for a moment. "Well, I guess I'll throw it back," he said, still cheerful. "Call me when dinner is ready. I'm going back out to catch some more fish."

We had an excellent dinner followed by a relaxing, quiet evening. Jason popped in and out, showing us the small fish he was catching. He didn't stop until well after sunset, and even then his engine was racing and he wanted more action. At about ten o'clock, several pickups drove by and pulled off the road near the stream. Jason went out to investigate and came rushing back in a few minutes holding a sixteen-inch carplike fish. He brought the dripping fish over to the bed where Linda and I lay in our pajamas. "Look! Look what I caught! The guys are shining their headlights on the stream. They know the shallows where the fish go at night. I caught this with my bare hands."

As he held the fish out to us, Linda grimaced.

"That's a nice one, Jason," I said. "What are you going to do with it?"

"We'll cook it and eat it," he answered.

"It's a tremendous fish, Jason, but we already ate and I think that type of fish is filled with bones. We're going to go to bed soon anyway."

"Oh, okay, then I'll put it back and catch another one." He ran off and stayed out for a couple more hours in his new adventure. He returned thoroughly satisfied with the day's achievements.

We got up late on Sunday and had a tremendous feast of eggs, bacon, and orange juice. We packed and walked to the main house to return the key. Linda went inside alone and the women all hugged her and told her how wonderful it was to have met her. They invited us to come back again soon.

On the drive back I realized what a great trip it had been for all of us. We hadn't had a wonderful family experience like that in a long time, if ever. The cycle of our giving and receiving was being established in our family, and it was making us all happier, better people. As I turned onto our road an explosion of color greeted me. A wall of mountain laurels with clusters of gleaming, pink flowers had fully bloomed. I sighed in thorough comfort that I was finally home.

ELEVEN

LED BY THE SPIRIT

Monday morning I went back on schedule, sitting on the couch, reading, reflecting on the words of God, and praying. I was led to the story of Paul's conversion. When he saw Jesus, he was struck down and blinded by an exceedingly bright light. Paul called Jesus Lord and asked Him what He wanted Paul to do. Jesus told him to go to the city. In a few days, Jesus told another man to go to Paul and put his hands on Paul, and Paul would be healed, his sight restored.

I read the passage over several times, then asked the Holy Spirit to clarify. It seemed to me that Paul was humbled or broken by his initial contact with Jesus. Then he was healed. I recognized the pattern with which God had worked on me. I had been humbled and then healed. Paul then came to hear God's voice very clearly and was led to help many people. Perhaps that was the next step for me.

I thought some more about the bright light. The light was so strong that it blinded Paul, yet he didn't cower in fear. He asked Jesus what He wanted. I sensed that Jesus' full light is so strong that we couldn't stand it. We would be disintegrated by His full light, and Paul, who received a strong initial revelation, was actually blinded. Yet he was cooperative rather than afraid, feeling awesome respect for Jesus.

I felt that my daily contacts with Jesus had been growing progressively more intense, and I was shifting from the image of Jesus as a friend, to Jesus Christ my Healer, to Jesus Christ the Lord, King of Kings. Although I felt strongly that the friendship was most important, the change of the image seemed a natural progression. Yet the words Lord and King carried a connotation of control I wasn't comfortable with. But whenever Jesus came to me, I always felt more free after the meeting, not more controlled.

Yes, He was certainly the Lord, but not a controller. He had the greatest power and authority, and by the majesty of His being He commanded—not demanded—the utmost respect and reverence. I felt His brightness, His splendid majesty flooding through me like lightning. I was simultaneously in His light, enraptured, and sitting on the couch in my living room. I stood up, giving thanks out loud. Although much of my time with Him had been reflective, listening, I had gradually been moving into a more active, vocal mode of communication. Now I felt my feelings bursting forth, unable to be contained. I felt as if I had been transported into heaven with Jesus and His Father. I had gained access to the throne room of God, and I saw the blood of Jesus sprinkled down the path to the seat where I could approach God under mercy and grace rather than judgment.

Jesus received the worship graciously as a great king would, but then He knelt and bowed His head, looking down to earth. He started to pray to His Father for the people on the earth.

I knelt down beside Him, my elbows resting on the scratchy couch. I entered into His prayer and felt the Holy Spirit stir me and quicken me into moanings and groanings. I perceived the grief and pain that people could have during their journey here on the earth. I was oblivious to time, caught in the rapture of God's presence. And then the Spirit said to me, "Go to Huntington Hospital and visit Jeff's mother."

I was shaken out of my reverie and found myself kneeling before the couch.

"Go," He said.

The voice was crisp, strong, undeniably real. I looked around to see if anyone else was in the room. Cricket, our eleven-pound Jack Russell terrier, was lying down a few feet away with her eyes half shut. This was very unusual. Cricket always left the room whenever anyone raised their voice, and I knew I had been making quite a racket. Yet here she was resting peacefully. The Spirit of God whispered to me, "She can sense My presence. She can perceive My peace."

I continued to look around, my thoughts racing. About thirty minutes had passed since I last checked. Should I just jump in my car and go? I remembered that somewhere Jesus had said that some people had done works in His name and called him Lord, but that they really didn't know Him. I wanted to make sure I knew Him. I sat down on the couch and became still. The practice was effective and my thoughts stopped racing. I said aloud, "Jesus, what do you want me to do?"

"Go," He responded.

"Where?"

"I told you. To Huntington Hospital."

"But what am I supposed to do?"

"I told you. Visit Jeff's mother."

"Yes, okay. When?"

"Now."

"Now?"

"Yes, now. Go."

"Okay, right, yes." There was more authority behind Jesus' words than there usually was, yet the voice was my friend Jesus'. He had something good for me to see or to do. I trusted Him totally, so I got ready to go to the hospital in a peaceful but highly anticipatory state.

I was soon on the road, driven by the strength of the "Go" and trying not to worry about what I'd do once I got there. I had met Jeff's mother about fourteen years ago on a visit to his home in Southampton. She was a nice woman. Jeff and I had been friends and roommates during our undergraduate years at Union College. He had been a good friend, and when Linda and I had been separated he'd asked Linda if she needed any help with anything. Jeff had also tried to contact me, but I hadn't responded. We had resumed our contact after the wedding, which Jeff had attended, and he had recently told me that his mother was dying of advanced cancer in Huntington Hospital. But what was I supposed to do for her?

When I got to the hospital, I headed for the front desk to find out what room she was in, but then suddenly veered off to the left and got onto the elevator. I pressed a button, got off on that floor, and went directly into a room around the corner. An elderly lady was sitting up in bed, back braced with a pillow. She looked weak and very thin, almost emaciated. Yet a peaceful aura seemed to surround her. I didn't recognize her, yet I knew who she was. We were alone in the room. "You're Jeff's mother, right?" I asked. "I'm his friend from school, Vinnie. God told me to come and visit you."

"I know," she said. "I've been waiting for you."

"I want to tell you about Jesus—"

She interrupted. "I know Jesus, dear. That's not why I prayed for you to come. I know Him and I know where I'm going." Consumed by cancer, she was so peaceful and sure that she blew my mind. This was way beyond any death and dying stage that I knew about. "I told God that I couldn't go until I was sure that someone would pray for Jeff. He doesn't believe, you know. I won't go until I know that someone will pray for him."

"I'll pray for Jeff," I said. "I guess that's why God sent me. I'll agree to pray for Jeff."

I approached the side of her bed to hold her hand and comfort her, but she was fine, already in a state of glory. Her hand patted and comforted mine. She looked deeply into my eyes and we both nodded, our agreement sealed.

Back at home, back on the couch, I prayed for Jeff and was captivated for the rest of the day by the great peace that this dying, graceful lady had manifested. I was sure, indeed, that she knew Jesus.

I shared the amazing day with Linda and then went downstairs to talk with Jason. He was interested in the events of the day, yet more interested in shooting a game of pool.

"You wanna rack 'em or should I?" he asked.

"I'll rack them up."

He got a cue stick, turned on his stereo, loud, and came over to take his first shot.

"Nice break, Jason," I said. "You didn't leave me any shots."

As I was considering the possibilities, I was distracted by some disturbing lyrics in the blaring music. The volume didn't bother me, but the words did. I wondered if I was just getting old, but there was more to it than that. I was Woodstock generation; the music I had loved had promoted a bogus freedom through drugs and promiscuous sex—what a mess. But this song was promoting far worse than a mess. The lyrics were chilling, about killing and suicide. I actually shivered as the song recommended suicide.

I took my shot, a safe one sending the cue ball to the far end of the table. Jason tapped along to the beat as he focused on his next shot.

"Wait a minute, Jason," I said. "Are you listening to the words of this music?"

"I'm shooting. Don't talk to me when I'm shooting." He took his shot, missed, and it was my turn.

I stood my cue stick on the floor and raised my voice. "Did you hear what I said? What are you listening to?

"Aw, come on," he said. "The words aren't important. It's the lead guitar. Did you hear that lead guitar?" He smiled and, did an air guitar riff.

I smiled back, refocused on the game, and made a few shots before missing. "Your turn."

Jason was hot, running off nine or ten nice shots in a row. The deejay now caught my attention, talking trash, and then the next song came on, as demented as the one that I'd just heard. I walked over to the stereo and turned it off. "I refuse to listen to this garbage."

Upset, Jason missed his shot and stormed over to me. "What do you think you're doing? My music is not garbage."

"Well," I said, "I don't like it. I don't have to listen to it. Do you want to finish the game with me or listen to music by yourself?"

Jason tapped his foot a few times. "Let's finish the game."

We continued, and after a few minutes the tension faded. "What do you think about taking another fishing trip?" I asked.

Jason gave a whoop and spun his cue stick around. "Great! Let's go. When?"

"Let's go next week."

"Yes. Definitely."

I paused and continued slowly. "Jason, please don't be offended by what I am about to say and listen carefully. The music lyrics that you hear, especially when you hear them over and over repeatedly, can get into you, exert a strong influence over you, and—"

"Right, so I'm going to kill myself," he said with an edge of sarcasm.

"So you *were* listening to the lyrics," I said. "You know very well that I'm not saying you'll do exactly what the lyrics suggest. You know that depends on a number of other factors, including your self-image and your family history." I caught myself playing psychologist with him and shifted my tone to be more personal. "I'm very concerned for you, that you will be happy and successful. If you feed trash into your spirit and your mind, you will eventually get trash out. You see your computer over there? Your mind is like a computer. Garbage in, garbage out. What you put in, how you choose to program it, will determine what will come out. I love you and I want the best for you."

He nodded hesitantly. "I understand."

"Good. I'm going to help you. I'm going to listen to the music with you and set limits on what you can listen to."

"What?" He stared at me in disbelief. "You can't tell me what to do. You can't make me like the music you like. You—"

"Hold on," I interjected. "I did not say anything close to that. I'm telling you that I strongly feel that I need to be aware of the types of music that you're listening to and if I perceive that the words are going over the line, then I will not permit you to listen to that music."

He slapped the cue stick down on the table. "Right, and what line—what's your line based on?"

"Spiritual discernment," I calmly responded. "There exist various spirits: the Spirit of God, the spirit of angels, the spirit of man, and demonic or evil spirits. If the music gets into the demonic or evil realm, it will not be tolerated in this house."

"Tolerate, tolerate," he yelled. "And I thought that you were so spiritual and kind, but you won't tolerate my music."

"Pay attention," I said. "I am spiritual and kind; that's why I'm concerned. Being kind doesn't mean putting up with something bad. I can be a lot kinder to you by trying to teach you the difference between good and bad. I've heard other music you play with a strong beat, strong guitar. I've heard romantic lyrics, funny lines, stories about life. You love that song about the riverboat queen, and I don't see any problem with that. It's not a matter of taste or style. I'm telling you that the songs that were on today had an evil, demonic character to them. We—me and you, you and me—do not want those words in our spirits, and I will not allow them to be released into the atmosphere of this house."

He backed off, shuffled around. "Okay, okay." He stated halfheartedly. I felt he needed some time to think over the conversation.

We finished off the game and tried to refocus on the upcoming trip. I hoped we could strengthen our bond over the weekend.

The following day I received a call from Jeff informing me that his mom had died the previous day. After sharing my account of our visit, he concluded that I had been the last person to see her alive. God had guided me to help someone outside our family, and I was glad I had done what

I could for Jeff's mom. I have honored our agreement and keep Jeff in my prayers.

The next weekend arrived, and we left very early Saturday morning for our fishing trip. Linda and Jason dozed in the car as I merrily reviewed the plans I had made. We were heading towards Keuka Lake, one of upstate New York's Finger Lakes. This time we had a reservation at a motel that provided televisions, phones, and hot showers. I had made a few adjustments from our previous trip, and this one was going to be perfect. We could even rent a real motorboat.

We pulled up to the motel, and I watched Linda's expression. It would reveal her initial assessment, which was usually correct. Her mouth turned up in a happy little smile. "This is a nice place," she said.

We got checked in and quickly headed down to the boat dock for a rental.

"Do you know how to work one of those things?" Linda asked.

"No," I admitted. "Let the man explain it to Jason, and he can run the boat."

"Yes!" Jason said, surprised.

Jason received his instructions and we took off. In a few minutes we were well out from shore. The sun was shining on the water and the lake was beautiful, surrounded by trees. Jason stopped the engine and threw the ten-pound anchor overboard. We fished for ten minutes with no bites, and finally Jason pulled the anchor, started the engine, and sped off. He was in full charge of the boat, starting, stopping, and steering. After an hour of no bites coupled with abrupt, bumpy rides around the lake, Linda started to tire. Jason, however, was full of energy, excited by his power and the utter enjoyment of speed.

"Jason," Linda said, "take up the anchor. I think I want to go back. I've had about enough."

"Hold on," Jason said. "In a few more minutes."

"Now, Jason," she said. "Take up that anchor now."

He grumbled, pulled up the anchor with annoyance, and flung it into the boat. "Oh my God!" he shouted too late as the anchor went crashing into Linda's face. As it dropped onto the bottom of the boat, Linda's hands went to her mouth and she cried out.

I grabbed Linda and tried to get her to remove her hands so we could see the damage. Her fingers reached into her mouth and came away with the fragments of a crumbled tooth. Her left incisor, in the top front of her mouth, was shattered.

"Take me home," she cried. "Look what you've done." She held her hand out to Jason and me. "Take me home. I want to go home."

Jason and I were speechless. All my expectations for the weekend flashed before me and disappeared. What could we do? I silently shifted to problem-solving mode. Even if we drove straight back home, I didn't think we could get a dentist on the weekend. And it would be long trip back with a broken, exposed tooth.

"Please take me home. Get me home," Linda pleaded as she stared at the pieces of tooth in her hand.

"Linda," I said, "those pieces are useless. The tooth is all broken up. Just throw them over the side. Let me look at your mouth."

She brushed her hands together over the side of the boat and leaned toward me with her mouth open. "It's bad, isn't it? How bad is it?"

I couldn't lie. Most of the tooth was gone. "Yes, it's bad. The tooth's gone. But there's enough left to work on. At least it was the one that had that little chip in it."

Linda covered her mouth, rocking back and forth. "Oh no. Oh no."

"I'm sorry, Mom," Jason said. "I'm sorry." He started up the engine and we headed straight back to shore. As Jason and I unpacked the boat, Linda returned to the car and sat alone in it, waiting to be taken back home. She couldn't even stand to be around Jason at this point. The pain wasn't fading and her emotions were racing. She had lost a tooth. She was irate at Jason for his carelessness. How could he have done this to her? She had a great dentist at home. He would fix it.

She found her breathing slowing, her emotions calming.

The whole vacation would be ruined now. She felt bad about that, but why should she? It was Jason's fault she had a hole in her mouth.

She wanted to go home, but she wanted to stay and salvage the vacation. She didn't want to ruin the weekend. But she couldn't think of any other solution but to go home. She didn't think she could get through the weekend like this. Linda prayed.

Before Jason and I got into the car, I told him that the vacation was over and we were going to go home. He didn't put up a fight. When I got into the car, I was surprised by the change that had come over Linda. Before she had been livid, and her mouth was in excruciating pain; now she was calm, her body normal and relaxed. The pain was dying out.

"I guess we have to go back," Linda said.

"Yes," I agreed. "I can't think of anything else to do."

I started back to the hotel so we could pack up our things. Linda exhaled deeply, and I glanced over at her. Her shoulders had relaxed, her head had come up, and her face was totally slack. She turned to me, and I could actually feel the peace emanating from her. "I just had this flash. The Holy Spirit sent me this image of a yellow Victorian house. It's somewhere in the town. We have to go there."

"What's there?" I asked.

Linda smiled, revealing the hole in her mouth. "I don't know. But we have to go there. Take the road into town."

In the rearview mirror I exchanged glances with Jason, who was still very upset.

I turned toward town, not sure what to expect. "Jason, we forgive you. It was an accident. We know that. Isn't that right, Linda?"

"I forgive him," Linda said, "but if he'd just listened to me in the first place it never would have happened."

"Stop," I implored. "Jason, you don't have to remain guilty. Tell her you're sorry and apologize."

"Mom, I'm very sorry," Jason said. "I apologize. I didn't mean to do it, but it was my fault. I was angry and annoyed, and that's why it happened."

"Linda, can you tell him again that you forgive him?"

Linda turned to look back at Jason. "I forgive you Jason," she said in a matter-of-fact tone. "I do forgive you." She turned back to the front. "Keep going, Vin. It's right up the road on the right side." She blurted out excitedly, "There, there it is!"

On the right was a stately Victorian house, tastefully restored with magnificently manicured landscaping. I pulled slowly into the driveway, feeling like an intruder.

"There's a sign next to the door," she said. "Can you read what it says?"

I pulled up further, and Jason yelled out, "It's a dentist! It's a dentist's office!"

We all piled out of the car and up the porch steps. Linda

tried the doorknob; it was locked. She was discouraged, but Jason wasn't ready to give up.

"If God led you to come here, don't you think that there's a dentist inside?"

We knocked on the door, then quickly progressed to pounding. There was no response. Now I was getting discouraged.

"Let's write down his name anyway," Jason suggested. "Maybe we can get his phone number and call him."

Linda wrote down his name and we went to find a phone booth. She reached the dentist at home, explained her situation, and he agreed to meet her at the office in ten minutes. Ten minutes later, we pulled back into the driveway and the dentist pulled in behind us.

He was a young, well-groomed fellow in yuppie casual clothes. "You were lucky to reach me," he said. "I'm usually not home on Saturdays."

He brought us into the office, which was clean, modern, and spacious. After examining Linda, he explained that the tooth could be repaired with a bonding procedure. It would take several visits. He could do the first treatment and then recommend a dentist in our area for the follow-up treatments. He went to work, focused, thorough, gentle, and personable. He was a great dentist. He even took our insurance, so we didn't have to pay anything.

When he was done, he told Linda she was very lucky to

have only one tooth damaged. It would be better than new when they were done with the treatments.

Linda thanked him deeply, and we left feeling victorious. We had stood together as a team and not given up.

I asked Linda, "Do you want to go home?"

"No," she said. "I don't see why we should go home. I don't want to go out on that boat again, but I don't see any reason to go home."

We went out to a fabulous dinner that night in a small local restaurant. Linda and I shared a faultless crisp duck in raspberry sauce topped off with a luscious, light piece of peanut butter pie. She enjoyed the meal with no sign of discomfort. Jason consumed shrimp followed by a rich chocolate mousse. In a few casual exchanges, our waitress revealed to us that she had just returned to her hometown from "the fast lane." She'd had a terrible experience with the man she'd lived with. It seemed obvious she needed to talk about this, and we encouraged her to tell her story.

Her boyfriend had discovered God and then broke up with her, believing that their relationship was sinful. He had tried to jam God down her throat, and when she wouldn't go along he'd become frustrated and left her. She'd become jealous and angry at God for taking him away from her. She believed that God's way was punishing her by taking things away.

We began to tell her about our experiences with God,

and she was soon sitting down with us, fascinated. Linda told her the whole experience with the tooth. Linda glowed as she shared for more than an hour about the mercy and goodness of God. The waitress seemed to relax as she spoke to us and asked us many questions. After a while the owners, a husband and wife, joined us too. Before we knew it, closing time had arrived. The waitress seemed more at peace with herself and thanked us for coming. It crossed my mind that if we had gone home earlier that day, we never would have met her.

We enjoyed the rest of the weekend. Jason caught several small mouth bass the next day, and we grilled them outside over a fire. "This is really livin', Vin," Jason said as we ate the sweet, white bass.

On the ride home Jason and Linda dozed while I thought about what had happened. We'd had a great weekend. God had outdone himself this time. He had led Linda to a great dentist that was even on our insurance plan. If we'd become caught up in the emotion of the accident, we would have missed His voice. He had restored our unity and peace. And we had all worked together. Jason had been the key to our success, which had allowed him to redeem himself. If he hadn't persisted, we could have blown it. We had to follow through, never give up. And with God's leading and guidance, we had.

TWELVE

VOWS

We were doing pretty well. Not only was I being transformed, but the family as a unit was being transformed. I felt as if God was leading us down the path toward Him. Jason's court date had come up, and he'd been let off with a warning because this was his first offense. I felt that he'd learned his lesson and that our relationship was beginning to grow. Linda's flashbacks appeared to have stopped. Based on her recent behavior accompanied by consistent peace and joy, it seemed she had finally been healed. I too believed I'd been healed and judged my first few attempts at reaching out to others a success. Jason, Linda, and I were free, healthy, happy, and united.

One night, as I turned the bedroom lights out, Linda cautiously said, "You know, Vin, I think that I would like to have a little girl."

I snapped up in bed. "What? Are you kidding? Now that Jason is a teenager you want to have another child?" I was extremely surprised, because I had raised the idea years before, and Linda had made it absolutely clear that under no circumstances would she consider having another child. I had accepted this and made myself content with one child.

"You know," she continued, "I had a very difficult first marriage, and having Jason was a very, very difficult birth, during which I almost died. I've always tied the two together. I vowed that I'd never get married again and I'd never have another child."

"Oh." I turned toward her. "I didn't quite know what your reasoning was."

Her calm voice came out of the night. "I was too scared to ever think of going through those things again. I had to make that vow to myself just so I could go on with my life. But now I'm married. Jesus healed me of my fears and lack of trust, and I can see that this decision not to have children is part of the same fear. Jesus is taking care of it."

"What do you mean?"

"When you left me, I was in such intense pain I opened my heart totally to God. I gave Him my pain and my fears and all those past vows. They were created by my fear, but Jesus is the opposite of fear. He's love. His love casts out the fear. I trusted Him to allow you back into my heart. I love you."

I put my hand on her shoulder. "I love you."

"It's just natural out of our love to have a child. The fears and obstacles about marriage and children are gone. If I look around, if I look inside, the barriers are gone." She put her hand on mine.

This seemed to be the final sign that Linda's healing was complete. While I rejoiced in that, at the same time I felt her plans conflicting with those that I had been formulating. My agenda had been to work on my relationship with God, then Linda, then Jason, and I'd been considering my next step. I could return to the work force, undergo formal training in spiritual matters, and possibly integrate spiritual principles into a mainstream clinical practice. But how did a child fit into all that? I wasn't sure, but I didn't want to ruin the moment. "I'm happy for you, honey. But are you sure you want a child?"

"Yes, I want a little girl."

I took my hand back. "What about your medical problems?" Linda had been experiencing very irregular menstrual cycles for years, at times going for months with no cycle at all. The doctors had told her it would be very difficult for her to have a child.

"Actually," she said, "Doctor Gorospe at work suggested I go for testing. I made an appointment at Nassau Medical Center for tests, and they said they might be able to set me up on medication that could sort of jump-start me back onto regular cycles."

I felt a slight irritation that she'd done this all before talking to me, but I pushed that selfish emotion away, instead focusing on how important this must be to Linda. And perhaps it should be important to me too. After all, I had wanted a child before. Just because this wasn't my idea didn't mean it wasn't a good one. Perhaps this was the next step in my plan. The more I thought about it, the more right it seemed. "Good," I said. "When are you going?"

"This Wednesday."

"I hope everything will be all right." I leaned down and hugged her.

On Wednesday, Linda returned home from the doctor's with a determined, problem-solving look. She found me in the living room. "I've got good news and bad news," she said, sitting beside me on the couch. "They need to get my blood work from the lab for confirmation, but they think that the condition is treatable with a medication that has minor side effects."

"That's good news," I said. I'd thought about the idea more, and while I still wasn't sure it was the perfect next step for us, I'd decided to wait and see what the doctors thought.

"I'll know definitely in a few days. The medication is successful about one-third of the time. It either works well or it has no effect."

"I don't see any bad news," I said.

"I didn't give you the bad news yet." She looked away. "I have a growth that's causing the problem, near my pituitary gland. It's not malignant, but it's putting a little pressure on the gland and affecting my hormone levels. They said that the worst scenario is that it can grow—I don't want to deal with that now. The best scenario is that it won't do much harm, it won't grow, and the medication can override the effects that it's causing."

I was dismayed but didn't let on. I took her hand, and she turned back to me. "The worst scenario won't happen," I said. "Let's focus on the results of the blood work and see what our choices are at that time."

She gave a weak smile and nodded.

The blood work confirmed Linda's suitability for the medication, and she was put on the drug. Although the side effects, nausea and tiredness, were unpleasant, she stuck with the drug until subsequent tests indicated that the medication had provided no significant benefit. The doctors took her off the drug.

Linda was very disappointed, and although I still had mixed feelings about adding another member to our family, I tried to keep her from giving up hope. "The growth is not getting any bigger, and there's no reason to think it will. They didn't say that it was completely impossible to have a child; it's just very difficult. We'll keep trying." And we'd at least have some fun in the trying.

Linda was mildly positive. "Yes, we can keep trying."

One Friday night we went down to our neighborhood church where we had been attending services regularly for several months. During the service, the pastor approached the congregation and said, "There's a woman here who has received bad news. Have faith. I want to pray for you. I believe you're going to become pregnant and have a child."

I looked over at Linda and her eyes were darting between the pastor and the floor. She was excited, yet hesitant, and didn't want any attention to be drawn to her. He had no way of knowing that we were trying to have a child.

"Where are you?" He asked. "Stand up. God doesn't want to embarrass you. The Holy Spirit is gentle. He will never embarrass you."

I was captivated by his words and restrained myself from poking Linda to get her to stand up. At last she turned to me, her eyes desperately seeking out mine. She raised her eyebrows, as if to say, "Do you think that's me?"

I nodded. I could see the hesitation on Linda's face. This meant a lot to her, and to stand would mean opening herself up to the possibility of more pain and disappointment. Linda stood.

"Come out here in the aisle," the pastor said as he walked toward her. "I want to pray for you."

Linda slid out to the aisle and stood with her hands outstretched, trembling.

He placed a large hand gently on her head. "In the name of Jesus, you are whole. You will return to normal and have a child."

She returned to her seat, shaking. I put my arm around her. "Are you okay?"

"Something happened I think," she said. "I felt something."

We sat through the rest of the service in silent amazement. I wasn't sure what to make of this. We were getting ready to leave when an attractive woman around our age approached us.

"Hi, my name is Ceil." She shook our hands, and we introduced ourselves. "I don't want to bother you, but I was compelled to come over. I've wanted to talk to you before, but I always hesitated. I pray for people, and I'd felt that God had pointed you out and asked me to pray for you and your new child. I've been praying for you and the child that you're going to have."

"Thank you," Linda said.

Ceil continued, "I felt funny coming up to you, but after the pastor prayed for you, I was sure. I want to encourage you. What he said is true. I don't know him, and I don't know you; all I know is that I've been praying the same thing for months. For your child. It's going to happen."

A smile bloomed over Linda's face. "Yes, I believe it."

I was gripped by her certainty. The Spirit working

through the pastor and Ceil had demolished any doubt and supercharged Linda's belief that she would have a daughter. We rode home, freshened up, and settled in bed.

Linda was thrilled, bubbling with excitement. "I've had this strong desire for a daughter for a while." She beamed brightly. "I know it's the Spirit. Even with this medical situation I knew I would have a daughter."

"Really? How do you know?"

"I just know."

"You're sure?" I persisted.

"Yes, I'm sure." Her tone exuded a finality and unquestionable clarity. Linda was happy, unmovable. It seemed as though God had given her a promise, a vow, a covenant that He would give her a daughter.

I wasn't sure exactly what I believed on the matter. Yet Linda's cycle returned the following month and has been normal to this day.

In the days that followed our conversation I found that I had accepted the idea of another child. In my talks with God I realized that this was actually the perfect next step for us as a family. In our own way, we each had been humbled, healed, led, and were now being restored. It was time to grow, to move forward.

I sensed that another part of this was for me to return to work. I also wanted to undertake a Bible school program that would take several years to complete. In the long term

I saw myself with my own private practice that offered out-patient psychological services with a spiritual aspect. But in the short term I saw myself at school and with a part-time job. That would be more appropriate if we indeed had another child. And it reflected the priorities that I had obtained from God: to keep my focus on Him, Linda, Jason, and perhaps a new child, only then followed by work. I was not totally convinced that we would have a daughter, but either way this seemed the right path for me.

I was in prayer one morning in June when the Spirit of God said, "Go back to Long Island Developmental Center. Tell them that you're coming back to work. You're going to split an item with Linda."

The institution was large, and each position had a corre-sponding item number and title. To split an item meant to split the job. This meant both Linda and I would be work-ing part-time, splitting a full-time job between us. At first I was disappointed, thinking that after all I had been through God would send me to a place where people really needed help, like Ethiopia. Instead He was sending me right back where I'd come from. But the more I thought about it, the more sense it made. The people who needed me the most were my family. There was no reason to look to some exotic location to discover my purpose. There was need all around me. I could provide service to people in my own community.

"I'll split an item with Linda," I said, not even knowing

whether this had ever been allowed before. The idea seemed perfect. Later I discussed it with Linda, and we agreed that it would be great for both of us.

I arranged a meeting with the chief psychologist, a man named Sy, whom I knew well, and the chief of service over one of the in-patient units, Bob, whom I didn't know at all. Sy was a gentle sixty-year-old with a fatherly manner and a mane of white hair. Although he was not responsible for hiring, I thought he might be an advocate for me. The meeting was in his office, and I entered with a feeling of peace and assurance. Sy was sitting behind his desk, Bob in a chair with his back to the door. "Hi, Sy, how are you?" I asked, shaking his hand.

Sy stood up. "Hello, Vinnie. I'm fine. It's good to see you. Have you met Bob?"

"No, I haven't," I said, shaking Bob's hand. "Nice to meet you."

Bob nodded, remaining seated. He was a tall, slender man in his fifties, with grayish hair and a careful manner.

I sat in the chair beside him.

"I hear that you're interested in a position," Sy said.

"Yes," I said, directing my remarks at Sy. "I needed a sabbatical for almost a year. I've been spending most of my time on retreat, talking with God. But I'm ready to come back to work now. I'd like a half-time position. I'm going to split an item with Linda. I'd like to have a promotion too, if possible."

"What do you mean," Bob said, "you've been talking to God? Did you have a nervous breakdown or something?"

"I have a relationship with Him," I said. "In fact He told me to come here."

"He did?" Bob sat up straighter, moving subtly away from me.

I shook my head, impatient with his attitude. Didn't he understand that it was God's plan for me to split an item with Linda? "You can't hold that against me. Ask Sy about my work history."

Sy's confirmation was hesitant at first, but grew in strength as he spoke. "I have worked with Dr. Ruhl in the past. His work has been outstanding. He's received exceptional evaluations in the discrete unit that has some of the most difficult cases. He is one of our finest psychologists."

Bob shifted uncomfortably. "But how is this talking with God going to affect your work?"

"It's going to improve my work," I shot back. "Don't you understand? Having a relationship with God will make my work even better." I couldn't believe that anyone would actually doubt God's beneficial influence.

Sy spoke into the silence. "We'd be fortunate to have you back, but I don't know if a promotion is possible. I do know that you can't split an item with Linda. Neither personnel nor general administrative policy allow husband and wife to work together on the same unit. However, there are two half-time items available now, and you can take either one."

"You don't understand," I said, slightly annoyed. "I'm going to split an item with Linda."

"No, I don't think so," Sy responded.

I sighed, frustrated that things were not going my way. "Let me know where the positions are. I'll check them out and get back to you. By the way, are there any full-time positions available?"

"Yes, in the education and training unit, but I thought you wanted half-time."

I nodded. "Yes, I do. Thanks. I'll get back to you in a couple of days." I shook hands with Sy and Bob, who stood up this time as if glad to see me go. Then I headed immediately to the education and training unit to find out who was in charge. I found out that Tony, an old friend who had once attended graduate school with Linda and me, headed the unit. I tracked him down in his office.

"Hi, Tony. How are you?"

Tony had grown a moustache since I'd last seen him and was looking good. He was a big guy, but soft-spoken, very friendly. "Hey, Vinnie. Good to see you. It's been a while."

"Yeah. I understand that you have a position. I'm interested."

He smiled. "You are? Great. It's yours."

"Well," I said, "there's one catch. I want half-time. I want to split the item with Linda."

"Oh." His smile fell, and I could sense him backing off. "I think highly of both of you, but I want one full-time person."

I took a few steps closer to his desk. "You're kidding. You'd get more out of the two of us than you'd get out of any one person."

He rubbed his chin. "I don't know. There are scheduling problems, and the administration doesn't want husband and wife teams on the same unit. Why don't you take the position?"

"No thanks. Thanks anyway. It's been nice to see you." I made my good-byes confidently, inwardly perplexed that God's plan didn't seem to be coming together.

I went home to discuss the matter with Linda, which we did over dinner. "God said that I was going to split an item with you. I don't understand what happened."

Linda's hazel eyes met mine, full of trust and commitment. "I believe that God spoke to you. And it seems like a great idea to me. But sometimes God's plans aren't so simple. What do think your next step is?"

"I don't know. Maybe you should go half-time first. I know that God said that we were going to split an item, but He didn't say I should tell them. Maybe I came on too strong, but I thought I should let them know what I wanted."

Linda bit her lip. "I don't think I should go half-time if you don't have a job."

"You're right," I said. "I'll take one of the half-time positions, then you call personnel to arrange to go half-time. Maybe then we can work together somehow."

"Okay, but you call first to secure your position," she insisted.

"Sure, no problem," I replied.

I was hired to work in a severe behavioral unit at the far side of the grounds, and Linda put in a request for half-time work. We prayed and then let go, placing our care over the work situation into the hands of Jesus. We decided to take another short trip with Jason prior to my return to work and his return to school for the fall semester.

For this trip we picked Lake Chautaukua in western upstate New York to explore. Not only was the fishing supposed to be excellent, but we'd also heard good things about the Chautaukua Institute, which offered a variety of lectures, concerts, and readings that might be of interest. Jason, Linda, and I agreed to go for a few days in August. The lake was beautiful, the accommodations were luxurious compared to our previous trips, the motor boats were immaculate, and the town, Bemus Point, was a little jewel that contained some dashes of excellence with a good sprinkling of rustic, country life.

We stopped at a diner to eat and then headed out onto the water. Linda was a great sport, and as she climbed onto the boat, which Jason would helm, I couldn't help but smile, realizing again how far she had come. She had been healed of any negativity from the previous episode. The old Linda would never have gone out on a boat with Jason again.

Linda kidded, "Now be careful of that anchor, Jason, we don't want any accidents."

We caught some small fish and had a marvelous afternoon, joking and laughing. That night, Jason stayed at the hotel to watch a movie, while Linda and I explored the small town. We had a great time.

The trip was truly wonderful, all of us basking in the goodness of God in perfect unity. I felt that from the love I had given Linda and Jason had grown a plentiful harvest. We enjoyed our days fully, laughing and playing in the sun with no shadow cast by the unresolved work situation.

THIRTEEN

RESTORED

We arrived back home on Sunday afternoon. As soon as I was done unpacking the car, I took a stroll through the trail in the backyard to view my favorite flowers, Rose of Sharon, that were sprinkled throughout the path. I examined the colors closely. Most of ours were pure white with vivid centers of scarlet and crimson. Songbirds provided a magnificent background chorus. I reflected on God's unfathomable love and sensed His glory covering our home. I worshiped God for awhile in silent awe.

A few hours later the phone rang, and Linda answered. "Yes, this is Linda Ruhl . . . Oh, that's okay . . . Yes . . . Okay . . . Yes." Her voice lifted as though she had received a present. "Yes, of course it's all right. I'll tell him as soon as I get off the phone. Thank you." Linda hung up and turned to me, beaming. "You're not going to believe this. That was personnel. They apologized for calling on Sunday, can you imagine? They never call anyone on Sunday; the office is closed. The assistant personnel director said something was bothering her so she tried to reach us on Friday. She had to speak to us. She said everything went through. She wanted me to confirm my approval to go half-time, and you to confirm your approval for half-time in that other unit. But then she asked if it was okay if we split my item! She said for technical reasons it would be easier to split my item with you. We will be working in different units, but we will split the item. Can you imagine? I guess you heard God's voice after all."

I gave Linda a big hug, spinning her around. "Of course I did. Wow. It all came together. Hey, partner."

"Hey, partner," she said.

It felt so right. After the interview, I had questioned whether I'd really heard God's voice. But I had. I hadn't needed to be so demanding with Sy and Bob, though. And I'd been on the wrong track, assuming Linda and I would work on the same unit. God had said we would split an item, and that's exactly what happened. Maybe it wasn't the way that I had imagined, but we split an item. It seemed so simple now.

I remembered that in the past when God had spoken to me, I had always been very still and asked Him the how and when questions. I had been so broken and contrite in those early days, and so insecure in my relations with Linda, that

I had been very careful to get instructions. When God told me about splitting the item, I'd been so excited that I hadn't asked Him the questions that had helped me so much in the past. I recalled that my sensitivity was related to an inner sense of broken contriteness, and I resolved to cultivate that place of humility and ask God for as much guidance as possible before running off in excitement again with only a partial message.

The next week I returned to work, but our family life rarely included discussions of work. Linda was talking about her daughter, planning for the arrival of her little girl. I was going along for the ride. I agreed to let her pick a name.

"Sarah. Her name is going to be Sarah," Linda stated with certainty.

I admitted quietly that she must have heard from God, since she was so decisive about the name. Sarah was the name, no question about it.

Jason picked up on the reality of his new sister before I did. He had moved downstairs to the large L-shaped basement area, where he had taken possession of the recreation area and set up a nook with his bed and couches that would be ideal for entertaining a group of teenage friends. He came home from school one day with a beautiful wooden sign that had the name Sarah carved into it in a freestyle, flowing script. The borders of the sign were edged in a double bevel.

The stained and finished piece was actually simple and elegant enough for Linda to display in the house.

"Look what I made for Sarah's room," he proudly announced, handing the piece to Linda.

Her face lit up in a smile. "It's beautiful, Jason. It's very beautiful. How sweet of you." She gave him a kiss.

"We can put it on the door to her room," Jason suggested.

Wait a minute, I thought. *Now he's acting like Linda's already pregnant, and he's sure it's a girl.* This seemed dangerous to me. "I don't know if we should put it up yet," I said. "Why don't we wait awhile."

They both looked up at me, surprised by my lack of enthusiasm, and said, "No way. Let's put it up now."

I gave in, and we went to the empty room that used to be Jason's. We hung the nameplate under the stars that Jason had years ago glued on the door.

We enjoyed harvest time as the holidays rolled in. After Thanksgiving I found myself Christmas shopping for Linda in an upscale, handmade crafts store in Northport. I was pleased with my initial selections, two small pewter angels praising God, one with a lyre, one with cymbals. I was browsing through other small objects when I was attracted to a small oval box with an old print on the top. Inside was a small sewing kit. I examined the cover more closely. It showed a young girl with golden-red, long, flowing hair having a tea party with her two dolls and her pal, a terrier-like dog. The Spirit of God said, "That's what your daughter Sarah will look like, playing with Cricket. They're going to be great friends."

Slowly, like the opening of a rose, love bloomed inside me for this girl, my daughter, Sarah. I broke into a huge smile. "Is Sarah going to have hair that color, golden-red?" Linda and I both had darker hair.

"Yes," God answered.

She was so beautiful. "Can I get the box for Linda?" I asked.

I didn't perceive an answer and knew that I should choose.

I wanted to rush back and show Linda and Jason my find, but I reconsidered and decided to wrap the box as a surprise gift for Linda to open on Christmas. I hurried back and shared with Jason what had occurred.

As Christmas drew nearer, I noticed a difference in the way we were treating the holiday. All three of us were thinking of the season more spiritually. That aspect of the holiday had never been that strong for us in the past, particularly because Linda and I came from different religious backgrounds. Linda would always wrap presents in neutral-colored paper and would pass on sending out Christmas cards. But this year every Christmas carol, every gift, seemed suffused with the love of God.

Christmas Eve came and we decided to open presents after our church celebration of the birth of Jesus and a tremendous Italian seafood feast. I held the small box for last. When Linda removed the wrapping paper, she opened the box, saw the sewing kit, closed the top, and stared at the print on the cover.

"That's Sarah!" I blurted out. "She's going to have red hair—well, whatever you call that reddish-golden color there. She's going to be great pals with Cricket—see, they're playing together. That's your little girl God promised you. I believe that she's going to have red hair."

Linda looked up at me, her eyes shiny with tears. She knew that I was with her now, one hundred percent behind the idea of having a child. "My baby Sarah. That's one of the nicest presents I've ever gotten. Thank you, Vin. I love you."

By February, she had experienced a number of consecutive months of regular menstrual cycles. But then the month of February passed with no cycle. She went to her doctor and returned with the announcement that she was pregnant. Sarah was expected to arrive in late October. We celebrated, yet it was not the celebration of people who had just received good news. We had accepted the news about the coming child much earlier.

I was in the process of renewing Sarah's room. We had decided to keep the wood paneling that Jason had loved, but we sanded it, primed it, and covered it with low-glare, oil-based, off-white paint that would be pretty yet durable.

Linda was designing bedspreads, sheets, and curtains, and we purchased an antique dresser that needed painting and a crib with caning that looked older, classic. My mother was visiting for a few days and she watched me paint the dresser. Since I'd gotten back together with Linda, my relationship with my mom was back on track, and she visited often from Westchester.

"I think that I might want to go to the prayer meeting with you and Linda—if you're going that is." Mom didn't want to be a bother, yet she had a desire to pray.

"Ask Linda," I said. "I'll go if she's going."

"No, you ask her," she replied. "I don't want her to go if she's not planning on it." While my mother and Linda were friends, it always seemed as if they had to go through me in their dealings with each other. But lately, their faith in God had been drawing them closer together, adding a new dimension to their relationship.

I yelled loud enough for Linda to be able to hear me from anywhere in the house. "Linda—do you want to go to the prayer meeting today?"

Linda appeared in a few seconds. "What are you shouting about?"

"Do you want to go to the prayer meeting today?" I asked.

She shrugged. "Okay, sure, let's go. Would you like to go with us, Rose?"

"Yes, thanks," Mom answered.

There were about two hundred people gathered at the church. Somewhere midway through the prayer time, the leader asked, "Is there anyone who wants to break the smoking habit?"

My mother and several other people sprinkled throughout the group raised their hands. My mom smoked about a pack a day, though she didn't smoke when she visited us.

He suggested, "Someone next to you can pray for you."

Linda put her right hand on Mom's shoulder and raised her left high in a waving motion of thanksgiving. She prayed a soft prayer that only she and my mother could hear. For some reason we didn't discuss the event for the rest of the weekend, and I couldn't determine whether the prayer had taken hold or not since Mom never smoked while visiting.

She returned home to New Rochelle on Sunday and called a few days later. "Vinnie, I wanted to call you and tell you what happened. I knew that when Linda prayed for me in church something happened, but I wasn't sure what it was. I felt her pray. She was so sincere and trusting in God. I took a cigarette yesterday morning, not even thinking about what had happened, and it tasted awful. I spit it out and flushed it down the toilet. The taste of it was disgusting," she said, surprised. "But what I can't figure out is that I don't have any withdrawal symptoms. I don't have any desire to smoke or any headaches or anything."

"That's amazing," I said. "I thought that maybe God would give you the ability to break the habit. But He actually touched you through Linda and did it for you. This is wonderful. I'm so happy for you." I called out for Linda to come to the phone and share in the good news.

While they were talking, I reflected on the goodness of God. *Wow,* I thought, *He's restoring and transforming me, Linda, and Jason, adding to the family with Sarah, and now He touched my mom in a new way that I never expected.* I bounced around the living room, really excited, and shared smiles with Linda. She was talking to mom like one of her closest friends; the distance between them was gone.

FOURTEEN

WORK

By early spring the numerous forsythia were blooming in bright yellows along our road. I drove to work, enjoying the scenery yet focused on my professional situation. With my house in order, I felt I needed to exert some additional energy to my next priority, work, which had taken a backseat to family. I had recently been transferred to a unit that contained very difficult to treat, assaultive clients. Each had multiple diagnoses, the least of which were various developmental disabilities, the greatest of which were major psychiatric problems including paranoid schizophrenia, organic personality disorder, manic depression, major depression with suicide attempts, borderline personality disorder, as well as a variety of more exotic problems.

The patients were extremely volatile, challenging, and constantly asserting their rights. Several had lawyers and often threatened the staff with legal proceedings when any rules or guidelines for appropriate behavior were set. We were a developmental center rather than a psychiatric one, and that meant that we were supposed to be preparing our clients for the outside world, not keeping them locked up under high security. In fact, most of the clients went out during the day, and some even held jobs. We could not use straitjackets or other forceful means of restraint when a client got violent. I was blessed with an outstanding group of coworkers. I looked on the work as a healthy challenge that would tax my abilities, and I perceived the Spirit telling me that this situation would provide an intensive, hands-on training ground to hone my skills with the most difficult population that one could conceive.

I performed the usual psychological functions: testing, making diagnostic evaluations, creating specific treatment plans for all staff to follow, and collaborating with the medical personnel on the efficacy of various psychotropic medications that were often necessary and helpful. Yet informal interventions with the help of God proved to be outstanding, dramatic, and life-changing for myself as well as for many of the clients in the unit.

I established with the treatment team a reasonable set of rules and limits that would help the clients while they learned self-control. In the past the emphasis had been on punishing mistakes or lapses, while the new policy instead rewarded good behavior. This produced a mutual respect between clients and staff and a new motto for one of our repetitious clients, Mike Moss, which soon became a motto for the entire unit: "Discipline is not punishment, but the development of self-control."

One of our most challenging clients was Joe Russo. He had borderline intelligence and borderline personality disorder. He either bonded strongly with people or rejected them completely. If he rejected you, he could quickly become violent. But if he bonded, things could be even worse. He would cling with the constant need for approval, like one who had developed a "fatal attraction." Joe was a stocky, six-foot-tall middle-aged man, who weighed about 215 pounds. He was agile, extremely angry, and had huge hands. The first time I met Joe and shook his hand, I flashed back to sixteen years earlier when I'd heard Mohammed Ali at a talk he'd given at Union College. The one thing that had stood out the most about Ali had been the size of his hand as it engulfed mine in its grip.

Joe's hands were not only large, but the knuckles were gnarled. Several of the fingers had been broken because of his tendency to pound various objects and people. He had top rank in the pecking order on the unit and was considered potentially dangerous to anyone he had contact with.

Daily at about three in the afternoon, Joe, using his favorite shortcut, would come into the building and ask me to open the door onto the living area. The unit was a separate cottage, with my office at the front of the house. The main door on the side of the cottage was usually unlocked. When Joe came in the front door, he was actually entering my private office. There was then a second locked door that led from my office into the rest of the cottage. If he was behaving reasonably well, I opened the door with a friendly greeting. This was a special, small favor that he appreciated. Occasionally when he came in he would begin to rant, slamming tables around and yelling about institutional injustices. On one such occasion when he was especially violent, I told him to leave and that if he expected me to open the door for him, then he would have to act in a more civilized manner. He stormed off cursing. He understood that his anger was not being judged, but that he had crossed the line with some of his threats and his outrageous accusations.

The Spirit whispered within me. "He's been severely rejected since his early days. He's been abused verbally and physically, and he doesn't trust anyone." Compassion welled up within me. When he returned in about an hour with an apology, I went over to Joe and told him that I forgave him and that I wanted to give him a hug. He walked away in disgust.

I asked God if there was anything I could do for Joe.

"Yes," the Spirit said. "Apply to Joe what I taught you to apply to Linda."

I thought, *Well, I forgave him, I don't judge him, and I accept him as he is. What else is there?*

The Spirit said, "Dig down. Remember to see him as I see him, beyond his pain, and accept him completely as a person of great value and importance."

"Then what should I do?"

"Tell him that you want to take him out to lunch, your expense, no strings attached."

The next day I asked Joe out for lunch, no strings. He picked Red Lobster. We went the following day, and after a minor limit-setting agreement in which Joe promised no cursing or smoking in my car, we took off and had a great time. Halfway through the meal, he poured his heart out and confirmed what God had said to me. He was deeply moved that someone wanted to be with him and had actually taken him out to lunch. I acknowledged that it was a pleasure to be with a man of such value and worth, but then moved on to explain that God loved Joe and accepted him exactly as he was, yet God wanted to heal him, restore him, and let him know that He would never leave him. Joe cried and asked me to pray for him. We had dessert, and Joe grabbed a smoke, pointing out that our agreement had only been for no smoking in the car. We prayed together on our way back to the facility. As we entered the building together, he turned and grabbed me with a crushing hug of appreciation.

Joe and I are friends, I thought as I sat back at my desk. We had made a vital connection. I didn't see him as a damaged person, but as an equal. I'd never actually experienced this before. In the past I had thought of the client more as an object, an opportunity to show how good I was at my job. I had approached my clients with a proud attitude, thinking, *This guy's an impossible, hard case, but I'm so great I can cure him.* I'd always made a great show of my treatments to get credit from the other professionals on the unit. Now I was taking Joe out to lunch and keeping it all to myself. I really had changed, and I now had some power, with God's influence, to touch other lives in a tangible, significant way. I resolved to place God's ways first in every aspect of my professional practice.

FIFTEEN

THE FULFILLMENT
OF HIS PROMISE

By late August Linda's stomach was protruding notice-ably, and Jason made the suggestion that we take a trip while we still had the chance. We hadn't gone far from home for awhile because Linda had wanted to guard the new life in her womb. Although she was having some dis-comfort with the pregnancy, Jason was persuasive. He pointed out that the weather was cooler further north. We decided on fishing once again in Upstate New York, but with a twist. Rather than lake fishing, we'd try river fishing. We made reservations in Roscoe at a place that backed up directly on the Beaver Kill Stream, which was well known by trout-fishing enthusiasts. Jason and I agreed that we didn't have time to master fly-fishing, so we agreed to try our hand at catching trout using worms and lures.

The setting was delightful, right on the narrow, winding river. While fishing with Jason I reflected back on how honest and open I had become. My freedom enabled me to appreciate others more fully. I thought about some of the great qualities I saw in those whom God had placed closely around me: Jason, unbridled enthusiasm; Linda, integrity with a never-give-up attitude; Mom, forthright faith; Ceil, humility; and Joe, childlike in his enormous adult body.

Linda rested while Jason and I enjoyed our time together and managed to catch a few small trout.

Shortly after we returned home from our trip, we went to church one evening. A guest, Reverend Clark, was conducting the service. We had almost stayed home, since Linda was having back pains caused by the weight of the child. At times the pains were quite sharp, but we both considered these an unavoidable part of the pregnancy. Linda decided she wanted to get out of the house and attend the meeting, so we went.

Reverend Clark was a hometown, country kind of guy who exuded sincerity, warmth, and pleasure in his work. After he played his guitar and sang, he gave a simple message on the integrity of God's Word, and then he prayed for individuals. He continued for over an hour with specific prayers for people in the congregation.

Gradually he worked his way over to our area, his intensity so strong it actually felt like an electric charge in the air.

He came by our aisle and stood directly in front of Linda. "Young lady, would you like to stand up?"

Linda stood, her eyes locked on his face.

"You think that back pain is normal and you've accepted it, but you don't have to." He gently touched her back and prayed.

Linda began to sit down, and he said with a grin, "Don't you want more?"

Linda straightened up, her eyes once again locking on his face.

He put a hand on her shoulder. "You have been concerned about your labor. You have had a very difficult labor in the past. This time will be different. Your labor will not be difficult, and it will last less than two hours."

"Yes! Yes!" Linda cried.

He helped her to sit and moved on to the next row. Linda turned to me, her face filled with joy, and said, "I feel so good. I feel fine. The pain is gone. Can you imagine that! It's gone, it's actually gone."

October came and went, and Linda was overdue. On November 9, the doctor decided to induce labor, and we went to Huntington Hospital that evening to prepare for the birth. We had diligently practiced breathing and counting, and although Linda felt more assured about the labor since Reverend Clark's prayer, I knew she was still a little worried and I was determined to help her through this as best I could. After our brief exam, Linda and I found ourselves alone in a small room, working at focusing and breathing for about an hour with no results. I kept time with my watch and told Linda when to do the panting breaths and when to relax. Dr. Brown came in and gave Linda some medication that would accelerate the process. He examined her at five-minute intervals and kept shaking his head and saying, "No dilation at all. The cervix is not dilating."

Linda, who was becoming increasingly nervous over the entire procedure, asked between breaths, "You're going to give me that shot, aren't you? I want a strong local anesthetic."

"Yes, Linda, certainly," Dr. Brown assured.

"When, Dr. Brown, when?" Linda persisted.

"Soon. I don't want to slow down the process. There will be plenty of time when you start dilating. Then I'll give you the shot, we'll wheel you into the delivery room, and we'll have the baby."

"You mean *I'll* have the baby," Linda corrected.

More time passed with only some minor contractions, and Dr. Brown got up to leave with a puzzled expression. "I'll be back in a few minutes to check you. If anything happens, call the nurse."

"Wait, Dr. Brown," Linda called. "Aren't you going to give me that shot?"

"I will, Linda," the doctor said. "There's still plenty of time." He left.

I took Linda's hand. "We've been here about an hour and a half. What do you think is wrong?"

Linda breathed. "I don't know."

It hit me like a flash. "Wait a minute! We didn't pray. We got so caught up in things that we forgot to pray."

"You're right," she panted. "Go ahead and pray."

I hesitated for a moment and then softly asked God, "Please help Linda's cervix to open."

Linda's hand suddenly clenched around mine in a bone-crushing grip and she screamed at the top of her lungs, "Help! Nurse! I'm having the baby!"

Dr. Brown and two nurses rushed in quickly, and as the doctor examined her he said, "Oh my God, the crown of the head is out already! How did this happen so fast? Quick, take her into delivery!"

"No, Dr. Brown, no!" Linda screamed. "You promised me my shot! Where's my shot?"

Dr. Brown and the nurses wheeled her into the delivery room. "It's too late, Linda. I'm sorry. The baby is coming out."

Linda, her face sheened in sweat, screamed, "You tricked me! You tricked me!"

I moved along with the bed, my hand still clamped in the vise of Linda's grip. I really didn't know whether it was the prayer, the medication, or some combination of both—whatever, the effects were potent and dramatic. We got into the delivery room, and after a few pushes the baby was out.

Dr. Brown held it up. "It's a girl. A beautiful baby girl."

God's promise to Linda had been fulfilled. Her hand slid exhausted from mine, and for some reason I glanced at my watch—still thinking about timing the breaths, I guess—and realized that it had been about an hour and fifty minutes from the time we'd started. Reverend Clark's prayer that the labor would take under two hours had come to pass.

The cord was snipped, the baby was rinsed and wrapped in a cotton cloth, and Sarah was handed to me. The nurse said, "Look, I think she's a redhead. She has beautiful red hair."

"I know," I said. I touched the wispy hair on her head, and then brought Sarah's face to my lips, kissing the soft warm moistness of her.

I placed Sarah in Linda's outstretched arms.

Linda gazed at her with a love and light that enveloped them both and radiated out with joy and peace.

For thus saith the high and lofty One that inhabiteth eternity, whose name is Holy; "I dwell in the high and holy place, with him also that is of a contrite and humble spirit, to revive the spirit of the humble, and to revive the heart of the contrite ones . . . I . . . will heal him . . . I will lead him also, and restore comforts unto him."

—Isaiah 57:15, 18

CONCLUSION

Finding God, Finding Each Other reveals both the process and principles of individual character change, transformation, inner healing, relationships, and the marriage relationship in particular. Since the time that our marriage was saved by the power of God, I have incorporated the spiritual principles I learned into all of my personal relationships as well as into my practice as a psychologist working with individuals, couples, and families. For more than fifteen years the process within *Finding God, Finding Each Other* has been thoroughly tested and shown to be life changing across therapeutic settings: in private practice, in group practice within an outpatient clinic, in institutional facilities, and pro bono within places of worship.

I am grateful that I've found some keys to happy, healthy, loving relationships. Linda and I both strive for humility, forgiveness, divine guidance, and love that is kept alive by unconditional commitment with a never-give-up attitude sustained through prayer and action. Our marriage is awesome.

Know therefore that the LORD thy God, he is God, the faithful God, which keepeth covenant and mercy with them that love him.

—*Deuteronomy 7:9*

Dr. Ruhl received his bachelor of psychology from Union College, and completed his master's and Ph.D. in 1981 at Adelphi University with specialites in learning, cognition, and social psychology. From 1985–87 he attended and graduated from his community church Bible institute which is now under the auspices of Oral Roberts University.

Since 1985 Dr. Ruhl has conducted a successful private practice, worked with an outpatient clinic, and subsequently directed the clinic, The New Life Christian Counseling Center. For fifteen years he developed the use of Scripture with meditation and prayer as a primary treatment modality. He has had remarkable, positive outcomes with the restoration of highly dysfunctional marriages and has provided therapy for persons involved in some of the most horrifying abuse cases in the history of Long Island that have included murder, sexual abuse, as well as spiritual abuse.

He currently serves as an Associate Psychologist with community group homes where he exercises the admonition of Christ, "Inasmuch as ye have done it to one of the least of these my brethren, ye have done it unto me" (Matt. 25:40). He gives consultation to therapists and clergy on the counseling of hard-to-treat persons. He is a member of the prayer team for Glory Zone Fellowship, an affiliate of Church on the Rock International.

Along with his wife Linda, he has given marriage restoration counseling within places of worship in the Long Island region. They are very happily married and reside in Suffolk County with their wonderful daughter, Sarah, who is now a high school student.

Correspondence can be sent to:

Dr. Vincent Ruhl
P.O. Box 20118
Huntington Station, NY 11746-0851

Dr. Ruhl is available for readings from *Finding God, Finding Each Other,* with talk and discussion on the following topics:

- Intimacy with God through meditation and prayer
- Transformation of character
- Inner healing through forgiveness
- Restoring a broken marriage
- Building a strong marriage
- Death and dying
- Intercession

Workshops on these topics are also available.